Learning Piano

Learning Piano

Piece by Piece

Elyse Mach
Northeastern Illinois University

New York   Oxford
OXFORD UNIVERSITY PRESS
2006

Oxford University Press, Inc., publishes works that further Oxford University's
objective of excellence in research, scholarship, and education.

Oxford New York
Auckland Cape Town Dar es Salaam Hong Kong Karachi
Kuala Lumpur Madrid Melbourne Mexico City Nairobi
New Delhi Shanghai Taipei Toronto

With offices in
Argentina Austria Brazil Chile Czech Republic France Greece
Guatemala Hungary Italy Japan Poland Portugal Singapore
South Korea Switzerland Thailand Turkey Ukraine Vietnam

Copyright © 2006 by Oxford University Press, Inc.

Published by Oxford University Press, Inc.
198 Madison Avenue, New York, New York 10016
http://www.oup.com

Oxford is a registered trademark of Oxford University Press

Printed in Canada

ISBN 13: 978-0-19-517033-7
ISBN 0-19-517033-4

To my students and to O'Ryan
with joy and gratitude

Contents

Preface   xi

UNIT 1   *Keyboard Introduction*   *1*

Sitting at the Keyboard   1
Finger Numbers   3
Basic Note Values   4
The Keyboard   6
Dynamics   8
More Dynamic Signs   10
Using the White Keys   11
Using Black-Key Groups to Locate White
   Keys   12

Octave   12
Terms   14
More Terms   16
Improvisation   19
Rhythms to Read   20
Training the Ear   20
Worksheet Review   21

UNIT 2   *Playing Melodies Using Different Positions*   *23*

C Five-Finger Position   23
Time Signature: 4/4   24
Slur and Phrase Markings   25
G Five-Finger Position   27
Common Time Sign: C   27
Middle C Position   29

Rests   29
Time Signature: 3/4   29
Tied Notes   31
Improvisation   35
Technique   36

UNIT 3   *Reading Music*   *39*

The Staff and Clefs   39
Grand Staff   40
Landmark Pairs   41
Intervals   43
Seconds   44
Thirds   45
Transposition   47
Dynamic Changes   47

Fourths   49
Damper Pedal   49
Fifths   51
Upbeat and Downbeat   53
Rhythms to Read   57
Training the Ear   58
Worksheet Review   59

UNIT 4 *More Reading Basics*   61

Playing in Various Octaves   61
Fermata   64
Tempo Markings   65
Flat Sign   67
8va ‑‑‑‑‑‑‑¡   69
Sharp Sign   70
8va ‑‑‑‑‑‑‑‑!   70
Ritardando (Rit.)   70
Natural Sign   71

Staccato   72
Accent Sign   72
More Dynamic Markings   76
Improvisation   79
Technique   79
Rhythms to Read   80
Training the Ear   81
Worksheet Review   83

UNIT 5 *Major Five-Finger Patterns and Major Triads*   85

Half Step   85
Whole Step   86
The Major Five-Finger Pattern   86
Major Triads   89
Five-Finger Patterns and Triads in Major   90

Eighth Notes   90
Improvisation   98
Technique   98
Rhythms to Read   99
Training the Ear   100

UNIT 6 *Minor Five-Finger Patterns and Minor Triads*   101

The Minor Five-Finger Pattern   101
New Time Signature: $\frac{2}{4}$ 102
Minor Triads   103
Five-Finger Patterns and Triads in Major
   and Minor   104

A Tempo   105
Worksheet Review   109

UNIT 7 *Harmonizing Melodies*   111

Using the C Major and G⁷ Chords   107
Using the F Major Chord   115
Playing the C Major, F Major, and
   G⁷ Chord Progression   117
Dotted Quarter Notes   118
Alla Breve (¢)   121

Changing Five-Finger Positions   124
The Damper Pedal   127
Harmonizing a Lead-Line Melody   133
Rhythms to Read   133
Training the Ear   134
Worksheet Review   137

UNIT 8 The Major Scale/Reading in C Major — 139

The Major Scale   139
The C Major Scale   139
The Major Scale in Tetrachord Position   140
The C Major Scale in Tetrachord Position
  140
Playing the C Major Scale in Contrary
  Motion   141
Playing the C Major Scale in Parallel
  Motion   142
Playing an Arpeggio Accompaniment
  Pattern   144

Ternary Form   145
Intervals of Sixth, Seventh, and Eighth
  (Octaves)   148
Sixths   148
Binary Form   149
Sevenths   150
Eighths (Octaves)   150
Harmonizing a Lead-Line Melody   152
Training the Ear   153
Worksheet Review   155

UNIT 9 Reading in G Major — 157

The G Major Scale   157
The G Major Scale in Tetrachord Position
  158
Playing the G Major Scale in Contrary
  Motion   159
Playing the G Major Scale in Parallel
  Motion   159
Using the G Major and D⁷ Chords   160
Using the C Major Chord in a New
  Position   161

Playing the G Major, C Major, and D^7
  Chord Progression   163
Playing a Waltz Accompaniment Pattern   166
Harmonizing a Lead-Line Melody   169
Rhythms to Read   170
Training the Ear   171
Worksheet Review   173

UNIT 10 Triads and Chord Inversions — 175

Triads of the Major Scale   175
Playing Arpeggiated Chords with
  Alternating Hands   177
The Damper Pedal—Legato Pedaling   178
Chord Inversions—Triads and Seventh
  Chords   183

Playing Triad Inversions—Blocked and
  Arpeggiated   184
Rhythms to Read   187
Training the Ear   187
Worksheet Review   189

UNIT 11 Reading in F Major — 191

The F Major Scale   191
The F Major Scale in Tetrachord Position
  192
Playing the F Major Scale in Parallel
  Motion   193
Using the F Major, B♭ Major, and C^7
  Chords   193

Playing the Alberti Bass Accompaniment
  Pattern   197
Sempre Staccato   197
Harmonizing a Lead-Line Melody   198
Training the Ear   200
Worksheet Review   201

UNIT 12 *The Minor Scale*   *203*

The Relative Minor Scale   203
The Harmonic Minor Scale   204
The A Harmonic Minor Scale in Tetrachord
    Position   204
Playing the A Harmonic Minor Scale in
    Contrary Motion   205
Playing the A Harmonic Minor Scale in
    Parallel Motion   206

Playing the i, iv, and V^7 Chords in A Minor
    206
Prelude   207
Harmonizing a Lead-Line Melody   214
Worksheet Review   217

UNIT 13 *Exploring the Twentieth Century*   *219*

Blues   219
Windy City Blues   221
Transcendental Blues   222
Ragtime   223
What Time? Ragtime   224
Jazz   225
Just Struttin' Along   226
Twentieth-Century Classics   228
The Bear   228
Springtime Song   230
Scherzando   232

A Little Joke   232
Innovative Notations   233
15ma   233
Seashore   234
Metronome Mark   235
Quartal Harmony   235
The Cathedral in the Snow   235
Ensemble: *Black and White*   237
Improvisation   238
Movin' On Blues   238

UNIT 14 *More Repertoire to Play*   *241*

Four Miniature Classics   242
    Türk, *March*   242
    Köhler, *Melody*   242
    Kabalevsky, *Dance*   243
    Kabalevsky, *Moving Around*   243
Gurlitt, *Vivace*   244

Beethoven, *Für Elise*   245
Schubert, *Écossaise*   247
Joplin, *The Entertainer*   248
Robertson, *A First Nocturne*   250
Olson, *Razz-Ma-Tazz*   252
Keveren, *Wondering*   253

Glossary Terms   255

Assignment Sheets   257

Title Index   265

Composer Index   267

Subject Index   269

CD Track List   274

Preface

Learning Piano: Piece by Piece is written for a wide audience of individuals who have the desire to learn how to play the piano. The book is organized in an easy-to-follow piece-by-piece format. It is highly suitable for college keyboard classes of non-music majors, prospective elementary teachers, continuing education programs, and private lessons. For anyone who wants to delve into learning how to play the piano for the sheer fun of it with comfortable ease and rewarding results, this book will do it! And how will it do that?

The prospective student can look forward to playing music from the start—logically arranged with an easy step-by-step approach throughout the book. There are fourteen units in all. Material from each unit can be covered weekly—in addition to one week for review and examinations—in a fifteen-week semester. The abundance of material in each unit, however, allows the college teacher using this book to move according to class needs and goal objectives. In addition, the wide repertoire also allows the teacher to pick and choose—tailoring keyboard experiences in a fresh new way each time—rather than using a page-by-page approach throughout the book.

Reading pieces are included that offer a rich mixture of styles and multikey approaches. These help the student gain familiarity by working from one end of the keyboard to the other. There are repertoire pieces of varying styles, time periods, and levels of difficulty for in-depth study. A variety of ensemble pieces provides for team-playing experiences. All of these varied musical activities exemplify the theory and techniques introduced in each unit and all are carefully interwoven together. In addition, there are sections titled *Practice Strategies* that allow students to have immediate practice opportunities to enhance the theory and techniques introduced.

At the end of each unit various sections appear that provide the students with further opportunities to learn. For example, the student will discover the art of improvisation—namely how to improvise 12-bar blues, pentatonic and Dorian stylings, as well as open fifth and whole-tone stylings. The technique section contains various studies in aiding the student in developing good technique. The ear training and harmonization sections allow students to harmonize lead-sheet melodies that are most helpful in developing and training the ear. The ability to harmonize melodies is also valuable, since students learn to listen more carefully to what (and how) they are playing. Written worksheet reviews that can be torn out appear strategically throughout most of the units giving students the opportunity to reinforce, in writing, the techniques and skills introduced in the unit under study. Students also can write down assignments and other pertinent information on the *Assignment Sheets* provided at the end of the book.

Integrated within the units are interesting quips and quotes by famous composers and great (living) virtuosos, with most of the subjects having to do with some facet of playing the piano. In addition, a section called *On Another Note* discusses various musical style periods and topics as they relate to the piano, as well as short vignettes about noted composers. They serve to add interest to the music-making process and can be helpful in motivating students to take part in a musical discussion or researching a musical topic that may capture their interest.

The pieces that have been chosen and those that have been expressly written for this book offer teachers and students:

- a rich mix of solo and ensemble repertoire—including classical pieces from the Baroque era to the contemporary period, along with folk, rock, jazz, blues, boogie, and ragtime;

- a global perspective that features both musical arrangements of traditional pieces as well as newly created pieces representative of musical styles that are heard and played around the world today. Featured pieces include folk songs that represent France, Germany, Ireland, Scotland, Russia, China, Japan, South America, and Mexico; spirituals, hymns, and jazz and blues selections that have their roots in America; and mid-eastern tunes that weave an exotic tapestry of sound and harmony.

In addition:

- Unit 13 is primarily devoted to twentieth-century pieces, introducing students to jazz, blues, and ragtime; dissonance; clusters; polytonality; innovative notations; and whole-tone techniques.

- Unit 14 is a collection of repertoire pieces that vary in difficulty, length, and style—including classical pieces in original form such as *Vivace* by Gurlitt and Four Miniature Classics featuring the composers Türk, Köhler, and Kabalevsky. In addition, there are easy and fun-to-play arrangements of Beethoven's *Für Elise* and Joplin's "The Entertainer," along with contemporary pieces from Olson to Keveren.

Upon completing this book, students will have built a strong foundation of keyboard skills, techniques, and theory. They will have mastered some of the piano repertoire and will be ready to move to the next level of keyboard study.

ACKNOWLEDGMENTS

Special thanks and heartfelt gratitude to those individuals who contributed to this book in so many ways: Jan Beatty, executive editor; Talia Krohn, associate editor; Christine D'Antonio, senior project editor; Elyse Dubin, EDP director; Debra Fortenberry Nichols, copyeditor; Annika Sarin and Eve Siegel for their design contributions; Phillip Keveren, Jason Nyberg, and Ken Iversen for their musical talents and indispensable works; and Andrew Lidgus, whose beautiful artwork graces the cover. I also thank the reviewers whose finely tuned suggestions and ideas helped shape this book: John Blacklow, University of Notre Dame; John Ellis, University of Michigan; Barbara Fast, The University of Oklahoma; Joanne Kirchner, Temple University; Angeline Case-Stott, The University of Memphis; and my students for their enthusiasm and insightful feedback throughout the writing of this book

Keyboard Introduction

SITTING AT THE KEYBOARD

Sit tall and be sure to stay relaxed. Your arms should hang loosely from the shoulders and rather quietly at your sides, with the elbows positioned slightly higher than the keys. Both feet should be kept flat on the floor, although the right foot may be kept slightly forward.

This figure illustrates keyboard position for the body, arms, wrists, hands, and flexed fingers.

Hand Position

Your hands should be slightly cupped as if you were holding a bubble in each hand. Your fingers should be curved so that each key is struck with the ball or fleshy part of the finger.

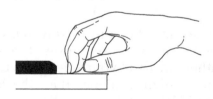

Fingers

Your fingers should be **flexed** as you strike the keys. Flexing means not allowing the first knuckle of the finger to collapse on striking the key.

As soon as possible, your eyes should look away from the keys as you play. Learn to develop a "feel" for the keys—that is, learn to play by touch.

Flexed (correct position)   *Unflexed (incorrect position)*

On Another Note...

THE BACKGROUND OF THE PIANO

The piano was developed around 1709 by Bartolomeo Cristofori in Florence, Italy. At first it was called a pianoforte because players could control the soft and loud (*piano-forte*) sounds. Later the word *forte* was dropped. The piano has had a central role in music since the middle of the eighteenth century, and has constantly continued to evolve. For instance, the piano on which Mozart played was quite different in sound and appearance than the one that Chopin played, right down to the pianos that are played today. The piano continues to be one of the most popular choices to study and play.

Source: Courtesy of the National Museum of American History

FINGER NUMBERS

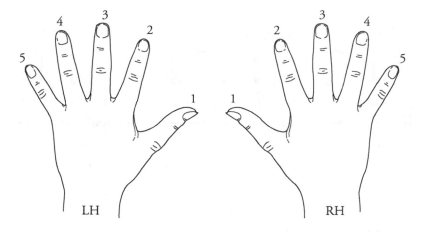

The fingers of the left (LH) and right (RH) hands are numbered as shown. Remember that the two thumbs are 1, the two index fingers are 2, and so on.

Tap your thumbs (1st fingers)

Tap 2s

Tap 3s

Tap 4s

Tap 5s

BASIC NOTE VALUES

Whole note	𝅝	= 4 beats
Dotted half note	𝅗𝅥.	= 3 beats
Half note	𝅗𝅥	= 2 beats
Quarter note	♩	= 1 beat

The combination of note values is called **rhythm.**

The recurring pulse that continues like the pulse of a heartbeat throughout the music is referred to as **beats.** Like a heartbeat, beats can move fast or slow. Beats are grouped together to form measures.

Measures may contain two, three, four, or more beats. The beats are counted 1, 2 or 1, 2, 3 or 1, 2, 3, 4, and so on.

Bar lines divide the regular beats into measures of equal duration.

Double bar lines are used to indicate the end of a piece.

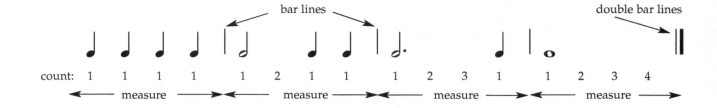

𝒫ractice 𝒮trategies

Tap the rhythm pattern combinations by tapping on the wood panel over the piano keys with the indicated hands and finger numbers given.

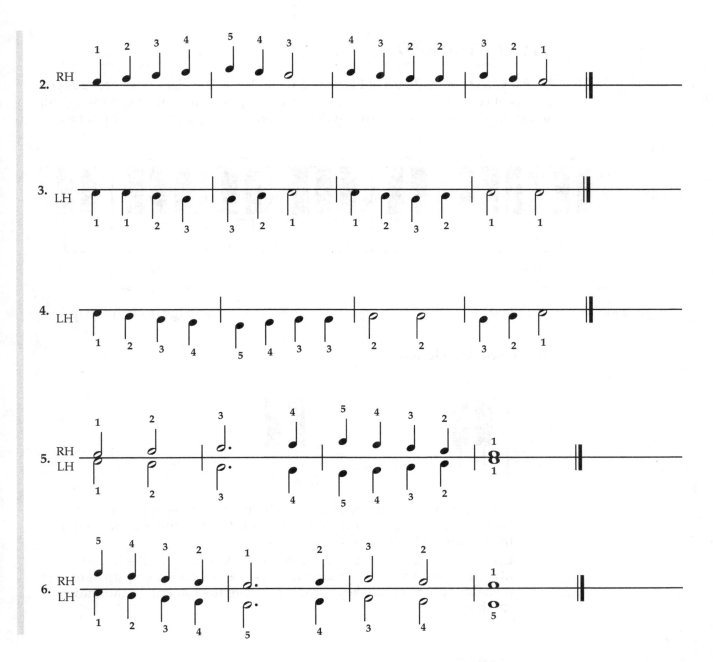

Van Cliburn *concert pianist*

On learning music: My first approach to the instrument was not digital, it was vocal. My mother [his first piano teacher] made me sing everything first before I played it on the piano, a method we applied even to Bach's Two-Part Inventions.

THE KEYBOARD

The keyboard is made up of black and white keys. The black keys are grouped in sets of twos and threes. As you move to the right, you will be playing higher **tones** or **pitches.** As you move to the left you will be playing lower pitches.

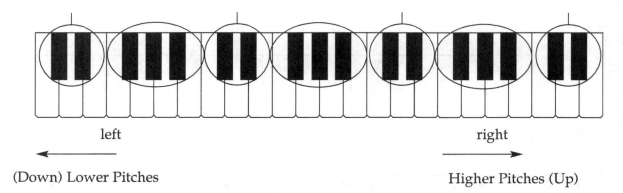

left   right

(Down) Lower Pitches   Higher Pitches (Up)

Two Black-Key Groups

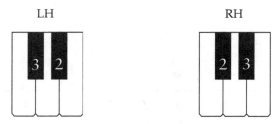

1. Play all the groups of two black keys (both keys at once) on the keyboard, both upward and downward, first using the RH fingers together, and then followed by the LH fingers together.
2. Use the right hand, beginning in the middle section of the keyboard, to play the two black-key groups (one key at a time) going upward and then downward on the keyboard, observing the fingerings and indicated rhythms given.

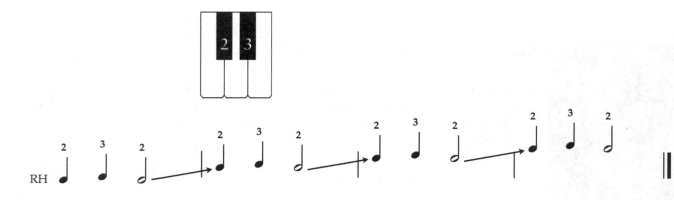

3. Use the left hand, beginning in the low section of the keyboard, to play the two black-key groups going up until reaching the middle section of the keyboard, and then going down, observing the fingerings and indicated rhythms given.

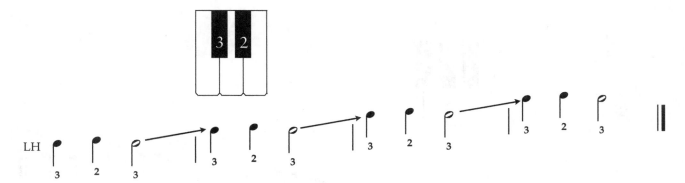

Three Black-Key Groups

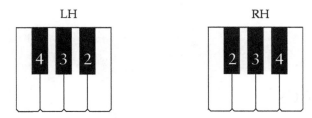

1. Play all the groups of three black keys on the keyboard (all 3 keys at once), going up and then down, first using the RH fingers 2 3 4 together, and then the LH fingers 4 3 2 together.

2. Use the right hand, beginning in the middle section of the keyboard, to play the three black-key groups on the keyboard (one key at a time), going up and then down, observing the fingerings and indicated rhythms given.

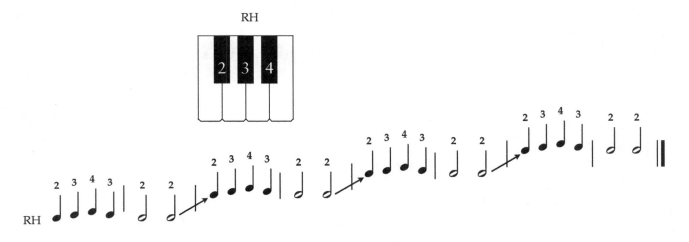

3. Use the left hand, beginning in the low section of the keyboard, to play the three black-key groups on the keyboard (all three keys at once), going up until reaching the middle section of the keyboard and then down again, observing the fingerings and indicated rhythms given.

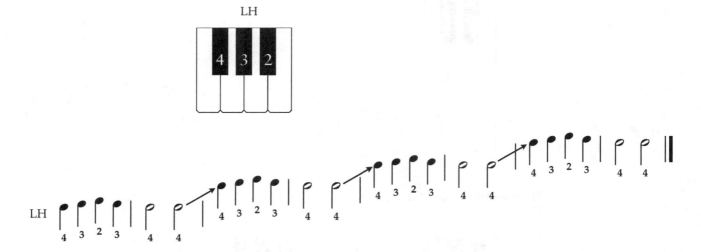

DYNAMICS

Dynamics are the degrees of softness and loudness in music. Two of the common dynamic signs are

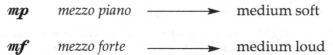

mp   *mezzo piano*   ⟶   medium soft

mf   *mezzo forte*   ⟶   medium loud

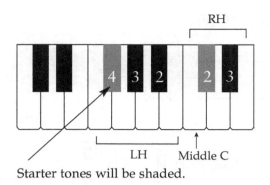

Starter tones will be shaded.

DISTANT SHORES

Elyse Mach

DISTANT SHORES

Accompaniment

Elyse Mach

MORE DYNAMIC SIGNS

$\boldsymbol{p}$ *piano*   ⟶   soft

$\boldsymbol{f}$ *forte*   ⟶   loud

Clusters
Play bunched tones together.   RH $\boxed{\begin{smallmatrix}2\\3\\4\end{smallmatrix}}$ LH $\boxed{\begin{smallmatrix}2\\3\end{smallmatrix}}$

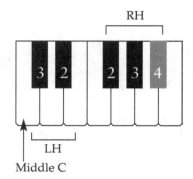

SOLO

SAIGON TRAFFIC

1:3

Elyse Mach

Steadily

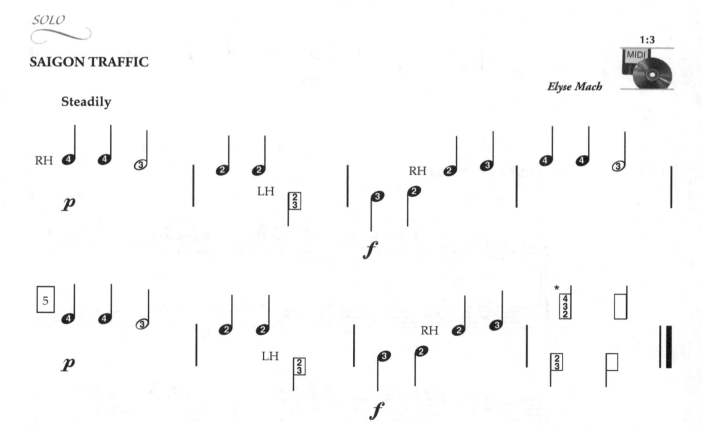

*Hold for two counts each.

SAIGON TRAFFIC

Accompaniment
Steadily

Arranged by Ken Iversen

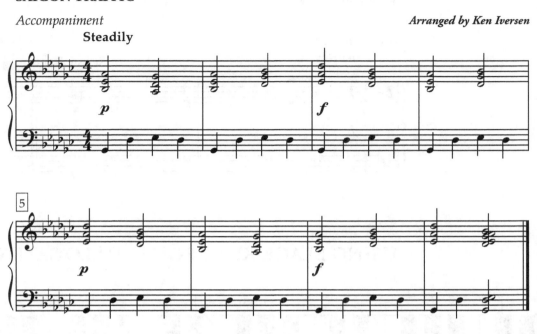

USING THE WHITE KEYS

The standard piano keyboard has 88 keys,* but only the first seven letters of the alphabet—A, B, C, D, E, F, G—are used to name the white keys, and they are continuously repeated. **A** is the lowest note on the piano. **C** is the highest note. Approximately in the middle of the piano, the **C** is referred to as Middle **C.**

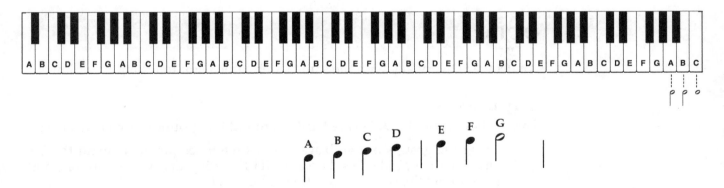

1. Using the RH finger **3,** begin with the **A** at the bottom of the keyboard and move upward until you have reached the highest key on the piano which is **C,** using the rhythm given. The highest and last three notes will have a change of rhythm. It will be helpful to say the letter names as you play each key until you are familiar with the names and location of the white keys.

*Some digital keyboards have fewer than 88 keys.

2. Repeat the same procedure using the LH finger **3.**

Accompaniment
Leisurely

Arranged by Ken Iversen

Repeat 7 times

USING BLACK-KEY GROUPS TO LOCATE WHITE KEYS

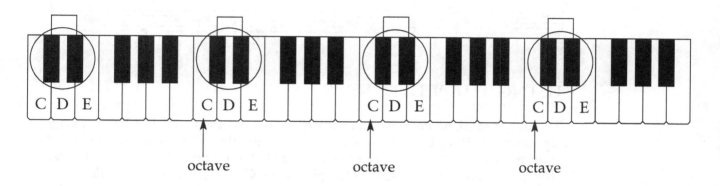

octave   octave   octave

OCTAVE

An **octave** is every key with the same letter name eight tones higher or lower.

C–D–E Groups
Three white keys—**C, D, E**—are located around the groups of two black keys.

1. Using the groups of two black keys as reference points, play all the C's and E's, then all the D's. Use any RH fingering that is comfortable, and then follow the same procedure with the LH.

2. Using the right hand, beginning on middle **C** with finger **1,** play all the **C–D–E** white-key groups, using the fingerings and indicated rhythms given.

3. Using the left hand, beginning with finger **3** on middle **C,** play all the **C–D–E** white-key groups, using the fingerings and indicated rhythms given.

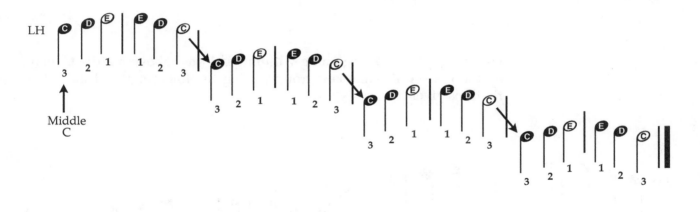

F–G–A–B Groups

Four white keys—**F, G, A, B**—are located around the groups of three black keys.

1. Using the groups of three black keys as reference points, play all the F's, then all the B's, then all the G's, and then all the A's. Use any RH fingering that is comfortable, and then follow the same procedure with the LH.

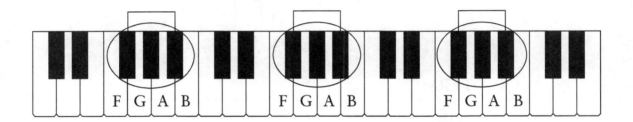

2. Using the right hand, beginning with the thumb on **F** below middle **C**, play all the **F–G–A–B** white-key groups, using the fingerings and indicated rhythms given.

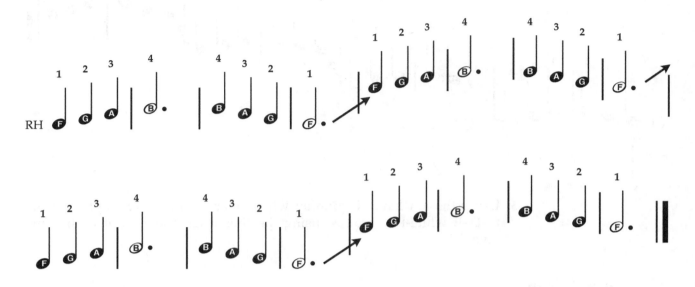

3. Using the left hand, beginning with finger **4** on **F** above middle **C**, play all the **F–G–A–B** white-key groups, using the fingerings and indicated rhythms given.

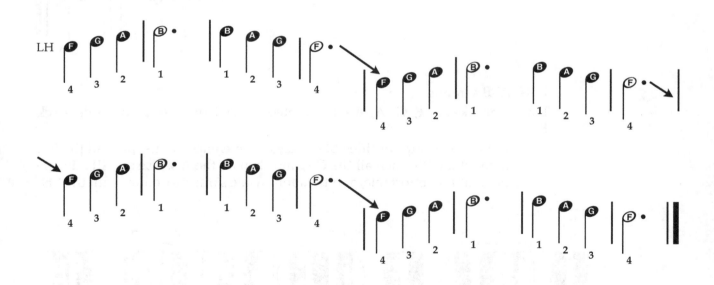

TERMS

Legato
Connect the tones so they sound as smooth as possible.

To play Remembering *with the LH— begin with the 5th finger.*

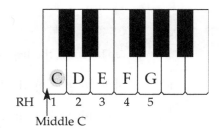

REMEMBERING

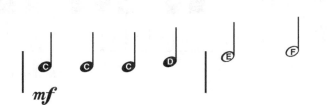

Elyse Mach

Flowing

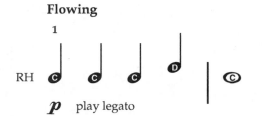

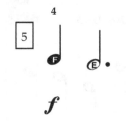 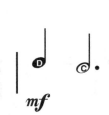 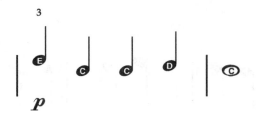

REMEMBERING

Accompaniment
Flowing

Elyse Mach

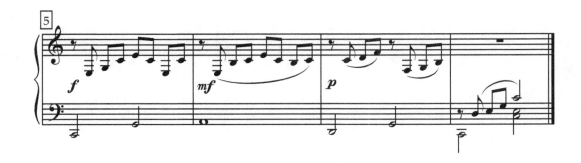

MORE TERMS

Repeat Sign	:‖	to repeat from the beginning of the piece
First Ending	1.	to play this ending the first time
Second Ending	2.	to play this ending the second time

To play Rock My Soul *with the RH—begin with the 5th finger.*

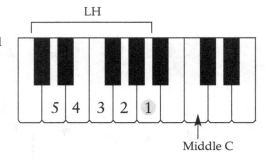

ROCK MY SOUL

Elyse Mach

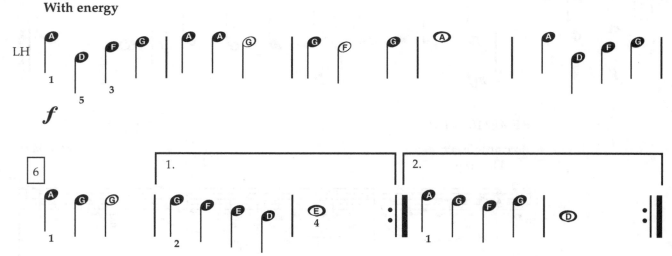

ROCK MY SOUL

Accompaniment

With energy

Arranged by Ken Iversen

Take turns playing different parts—experiment—playing each part in different locations (higher or lower) on the keyboard.

On Another Note...

THE BEGINNINGS OF MUSICAL NOTATION

Source: Courtesy of the Walters Art Museum

The earliest systems of notating music were developed by the Greeks between 1,500 and 3,000 years ago. Early music written for the Mass was known as Gregorian chant and these chants were notated in symbols called *neumes*, a Greek word meaning "sign." The earliest neumes were small marks that showed pitch in relative heights and were written down without the use of a staff. Over a period of time the neumes developed into a square-type notation representing specific pitches. A four-line staff was adopted, with a clef placed at the beginning to designate the position of the note C or F. Later a five-line staff became the standard norm.

ENSEMBLE

SAKURA

Elyse Mach

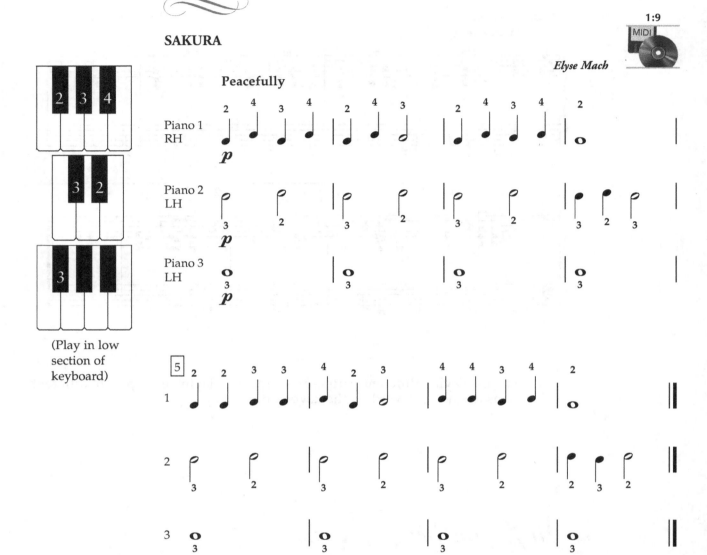

SAKURA

Accompaniment

Elyse Mach

IMPROVISATION

Pentatonic Improvisation

Using the **pentatonic scale** (a five-tone scale built on the black keys only) is a great way to begin improvising because there will not be wrong notes!

Make up your own melodies, using the five black keys only with your right hand while your teacher plays the accompaniment part.

Begin and end your melody on finger **2.**

Several measures are given to get you started.

Bouncy

Accompaniment   *Ken Iversen*

RHYTHMS TO READ

Tap the various rhythmic patterns that follow. The RH taps the notes with stems going up. The LH taps the notes with stems going down. First tap each hand separately and then with both hands together.

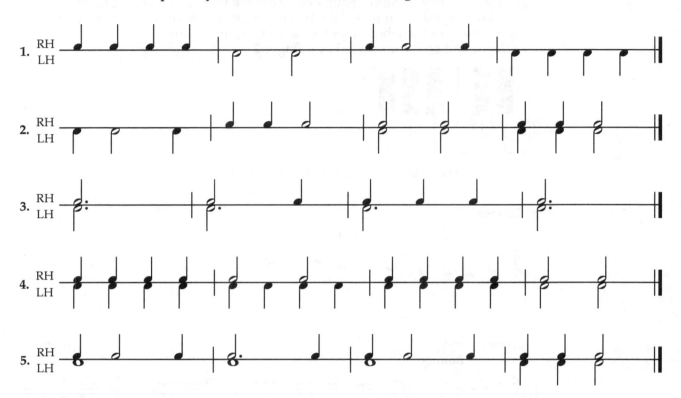

TRAINING THE EAR

Select the rhythmic patterns that the instructor claps. Place a check mark in front of each of the examples that are clapped.

NAME _____
DATE _____
SCORE _____

Short Answer

1. Write down the letter name for each of the checked pitches:

Construction

2. Give an example of the following note values:

half note _____ whole note _____ dotted half note _____ quarter note _____

Matching

Write the numbers from Column A to correspond to the given answers in Column B.

COLUMN A	COLUMN B
1. *piano* (*p*)	_____ an arrangement of note values
2. legato	_____ the ending used the second time
3. rhythm	_____ medium loud
4. octave	_____ medium soft
5. *forte* (*f*)	_____ the end of a piece
6. :‖	_____ to play smoothly
7. ⌐2.	_____ repeat bars
8. double bar lines	_____ soft
9. *mezzo forte* (*mf*)	_____ loud
10. *mezzo piano* (*mp*)	_____ from one letter name to the next higher or lower having the same letter name

Playing Melodies Using Different Positions

C FIVE-FINGER POSITION

Each hand uses the five keys—C, D, E, F, and G—
in two different places on the keyboard.

C Five-Finger Position

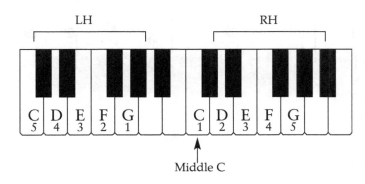

LH   RH

C D E F G   C D E F G
5 4 3 2 1   1 2 3 4 5

Middle C

TIME SIGNATURE: $\frac{4}{4}$

At the beginning of each piece there are two numbers that look something like a fraction; this is called a **time signature.**

$\frac{4}{4}$ beats to each measure

the quarter note (♩) receives the beat

PRACTICE SUGGESTIONS

Here are some practice suggestions for *Au Clair de la Lune* (and other pieces that follow):

1. Clap the rhythm while counting the beat aloud.
2. Find your position on the keyboard.
3. Play and sing the letter names aloud.
4. Play and count aloud.
5. Do not look down at the keys when you are playing.

First play *Au Clair de la Lune* with the right hand, and then with the left. The goal is to play *Au Clair de la Lune* with both hands together with no rhythmic hesitations.

1:10

AU CLAIR DE LA LUNE *(C Five-Finger Position)*

French Folk Song

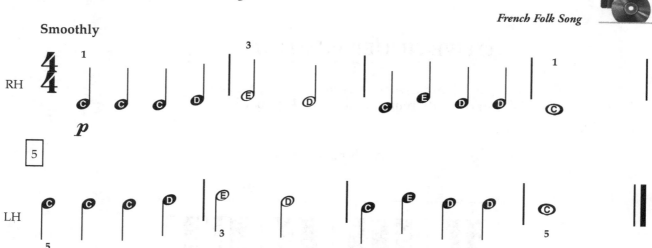

AU CLAIR DE LA LUNE

Accompaniment
Smoothly

Arranged by Phillip Keveren

p

With pedal

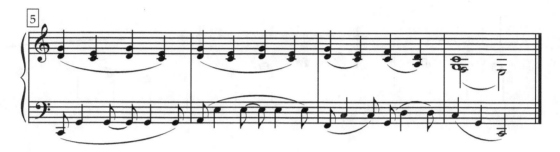

SLUR AND PHRASE MARKINGS

A **slur** or **phrase marking** is a curved line which appears above or below a group of notes. A short curved line is usually called a **slur marking,** and means that the notes within that curved line are connected. The connected finger technique is called legato.

A longer curved line indicates **phrasing**. A **phrase** is a musical sentence often four measures in length.

First play the first phrase (the first four measures) of *Ode to Joy* with the right hand, and then the second phrase (the last four measures) with the left, observing the fingerings given for each hand. The goal is to play *Ode to Joy* with both hands together in a legato manner.

ODE TO JOY

Ludwig van Beethoven
(1770–1827)

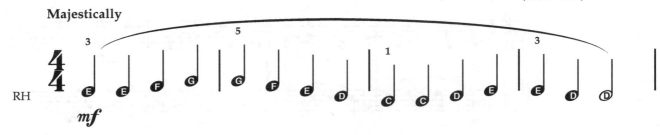

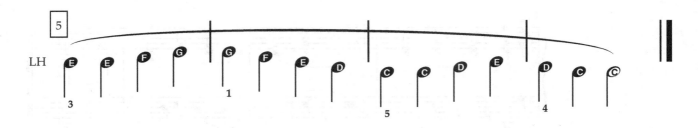

ODE TO JOY

Accompaniment
Majestically

Arranged by Phillip Keveren

On Another Note...

THE CLASSICAL PERIOD (1750–1820)

The music of the Classical period attached great importance to clarity, balance, structure, and emphasis on form. While composers still wrote expressive music, the emotions of that music were carefully veiled. The preferred keyboard instrument became the pianoforte (later simply called a piano). The melodies were usually simple, lyrical, and folklike, with the phrases mostly the standard four measures in length. The accompaniments had simple and transparent harmonies; a favorite choice of the classical composer was to use a music box style of accompaniment called the "Alberti bass." Sonatas, dances, rondos, and theme and variations were some of the prevalent styles of compositions written and performed. Well-known composers during this period are Franz Joseph Haydn, Wolfgang Amadeus Mozart, and Ludwig van Beethoven.

Source: Archivo Inconografico, S.A./Corbis

G FIVE-FINGER POSITION

Each hand uses the five keys: G, A, B, C, and D in two different places on the keyboard.

G Five-Finger Position

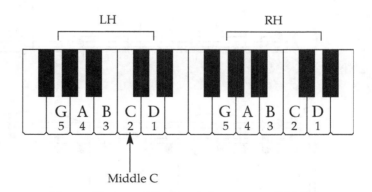

Middle C

COMMON TIME SIGN: C

C means the same as $\frac{4}{4}$ time, and it is called **common time.**

Play *Whistle Daughter* with the right hand and then the left hand using the G five-finger position given. The goal is to play *Whistle Daughter* with both hands together with no rhythmic hesitations.

WHISTLE DAUGHTER *(G Five-Finger Position)*

American

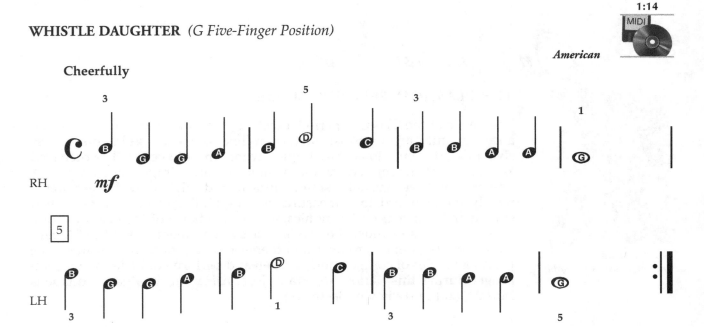

WHISTLE DAUGHTER

Accompaniment
Cheerfully

Arranged by Ken Iversen

Round

A **round** is a melody that is played with each new person (or group) starting the melody at specific times indicated. In *Whistle Daughter*, play the piece as a round by having the Piano 2 begin when the Piano 1 has reached measure 2. This piece can be repeated as many times as you wish.

MIDDLE C POSITION

The melodies in *Jazz Waltz* (p. 30) and *Shepherd's Song* (p. 32) are divided between the two hands.

Let the starting note and finger number be your guide in placing your hands in the correct positions.

Middle C Position

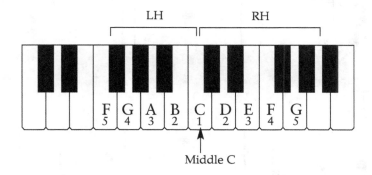

RESTS

Rests are signs that indicate measured silence. A rest sign is shown with the same value as each note.

▬	**Whole rest**	4 beats or any whole measure
▬	**Half rest**	2 beats
𝄽	**Quarter rest**	1 beat

TIME SIGNATURE: ¾

$\frac{3}{4}$ 3 beats to the measure

the quarter note (♩) receives one beat

A JAZZ WALTZ

Phillip Keveren

Remember to not look down at the keys when you are playing.

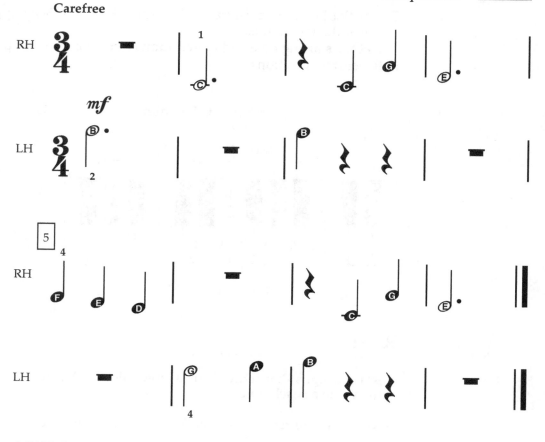

A JAZZ WALTZ

Phillip Keveren

On Another Note...

LUDWIG VAN BEETHOVEN

Source: Library of Congress, Prints and Photographs Division, reproduction number LC-USZ62-29499.

Ludwig van Beethoven (1770–1827) is considered to be one of the greatest composers of the Classical period. He also serves as a bridge to the Romantic period because of the Romantic style developments that he displayed in his later compositions. Born in Bonn, Germany, Beethoven first studied with his father, Johann who was a singer and instrumentalist, and later with such teachers as Franz Joseph Haydn and Antonio Salieri. He made his public debut as a piano virtuoso at the age of 15, and about this time his first important publications for the piano appeared as well. Probably Beethoven's *Für Elise* and the first movement of his *Moonlight Sonata* are among his most loved pieces for the piano. Recent research discoveries reveal that *Für Elise* was really written for a lady by the name of Therese, but the alias Elise was used by Beethoven to keep the real name a secret. Unfortunately, before Beethoven reached the age of 30, he was already suffering from an incurable deafness. Remarkably, however, many of his finest works were written after his deafness set in. When he died in 1827, ten thousand people were said to have attended his funeral. Beethoven has given the world quite a musical legacy with the richness of music he left behind.

TIED NOTES

A **tie** is a curved line which connects notes on the *same* line or space. Play the first note and hold for the combined value of both notes.

keep holding

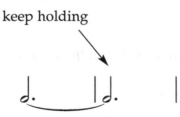

SHEPHERD'S SONG *("Pastoral" from Symphony No. 6)*

Ludwig van Beethoven
(1770–1827)

1:18

SHEPHERD'S SONG *("Pastoral" from Symphony No. 6)*

Accompaniment

Arranged by Elyse Mach

Dorian Mode

The white keys from D to D form the scale of the **Dorian mode,** which is used frequently in certain styles of jazz music. The first five tones of the Dorian mode are used in the ensemble piece, *Dorian Four*. (The last measure uses the sixth tone of B in the Piano 2 part.)

Play each of the four parts of *Dorian Four* using the fingering given under the notes.

DORIAN FOUR

Ken Iversen

Continued

*Use the left hand 2nd finger to play the B.

DORIAN FOUR

Accompaniment

Easily

Ken Iversen

IMPROVISATION

Dorian Mode Improvisation

Make up your own Dorian mode melodies using your right hand to play the white keys of D–E–F–G–A. Your teacher will play an accompaniment part to your melody.

Start and end your melody with the note D.

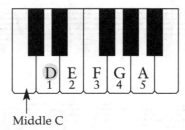

Middle C

The first few measures are given to help get you started.

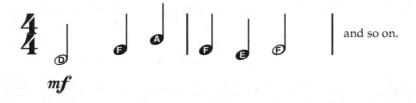

DORIAN MODE IMPROVISATION

Accompaniment
Easy

Ken Iversen

TECHNIQUE

Practice the following studies with the right hand starting on middle C and then moving upward to the C one octave above. Repeat those studies that have new fingerings given.

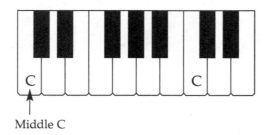

Middle C

1.

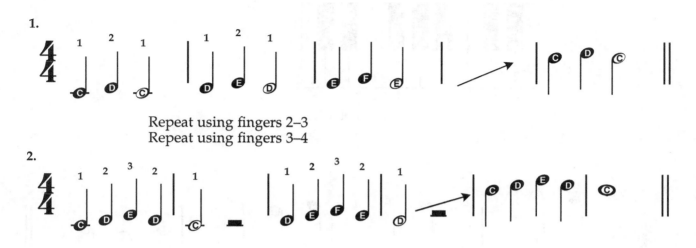

Repeat using fingers 2–3
Repeat using fingers 3–4

2.

Repeat using fingers 2–3–4
Repeat using fingers 3–4–5

3.

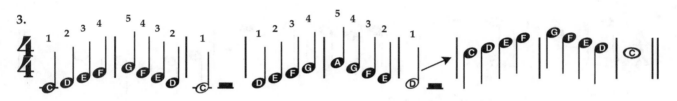

Repeat using fingers 2–3–4–5

4.

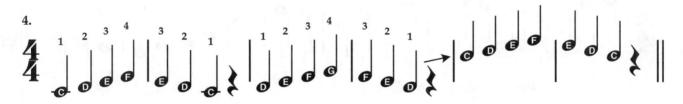

Repeat these studies using the G five-finger position.

Practice the following studies with the left hand starting on middle C and then moving downward to the C one octave below. Repeat those studies that have new fingerings given.

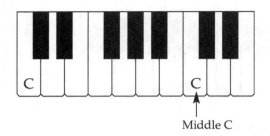

Middle C

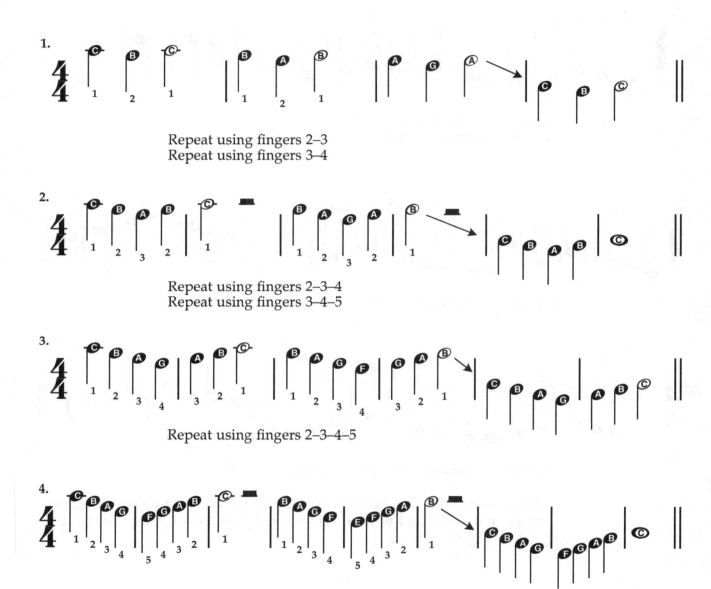

1.

Repeat using fingers 2–3
Repeat using fingers 3–4

2.

Repeat using fingers 2–3–4
Repeat using fingers 3–4–5

3.

Repeat using fingers 2–3–4–5

4.

UNIT

3

Reading Music

THE STAFF AND CLEFS

A **staff** consists of five lines and four spaces.

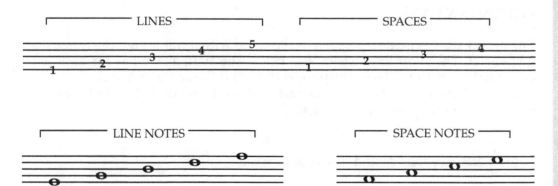

Treble Clef Sign

The **treble clef** sign is called the **G clef** because it locates the G above middle C. Notice how the G clef figure circles around the G line (2nd staff line).

Bass Clef Sign

The **bass clef** sign is called the **F clef** because it locates the F below middle C. Notice how the two dots encircle the F line (4th staff line).

GRAND STAFF

The **grand staff** is made up of two staves, one with a treble clef, the other with a bass clef. The short lines above and below the staff, as well as for middle C, are called **leger lines.** Their purpose is to extend the range of the staves.

The darkened notes (♩) are **landmark notes** which will help you to read the notes surrounding them more quickly.

In 𝄞 clef, use the **C's** and **G's** as landmarks.

In 𝄢 clef, use the **C's** and **F's** as landmarks.

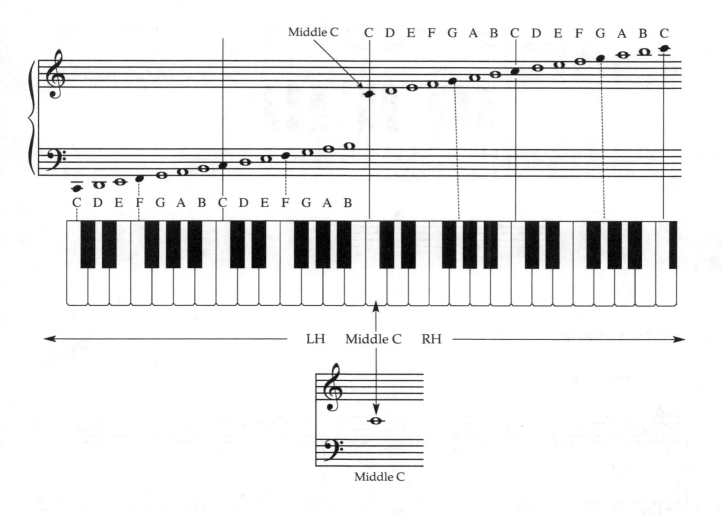

Middle C

Middle C uses a leger line and is found between the treble and bass clef staves.

LANDMARK PAIRS

The **landmark pair** of **C** and **G** will be helpful in learning the notes surrounding them when reading in **treble clef**.

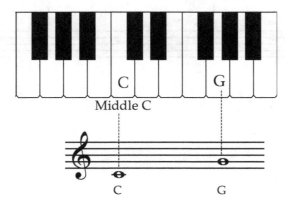

The **landmark pair** of **F** and **C** will be helpful in learning the notes surrounding them when reading in **bass clef.**

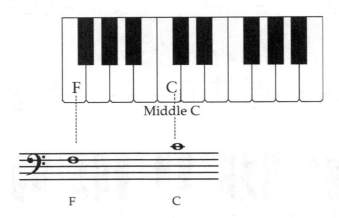

LANDMARK PAIRS

1:21

Ken Iversen

With energy

LANDMARK PAIRS

Accompaniment

With energy

Ken Iversen

INTERVALS

An **interval** is the distance between two notes.

* Neighboring white keys are a second apart.
* An interval of a third skips a white key.
* An interval of a fourth skips 2 white keys.
* An interval of a fifth skips 3 white keys.

Interval: └─ 2 ─┘   └─ 3 ─┘   └─ 4 ─┘   └─ 5 ─┘

Melodic Intervals
Melodic intervals are written and played one note following the other:

Harmonic Intervals
Harmonic intervals are written and played together:

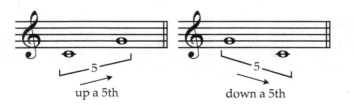

up a 5th   down a 5th

Practice playing the following intervals which are given both melodically and harmonically.

- Listen to sound of each interval as you play them.
- Feel the difference in the size of each of the intervals as you play them.

SECONDS

A **second** is from **a line note to the next space note above or below it, OR a space note to the next line note above or below it.**

Notice that *Stepping Along* uses intervals of a second for much of the melody.

1:23

STEPPING ALONG

Elyse Mach

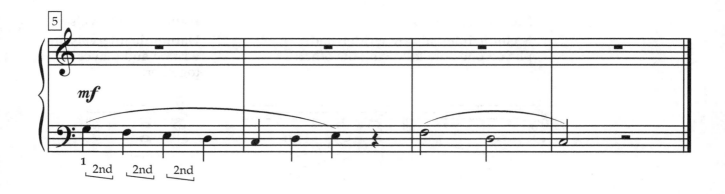

STEPPING ALONG

Accompaniment
Marchlike   *Arranged by Phillip Keveren*

THIRDS

Thirds move from **one line to the next line, either up or down, OR from one space to the next space, either up or down.**

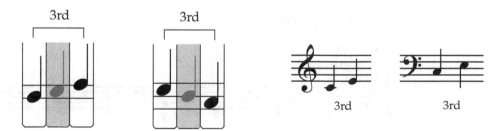

Pick out the intervals of a third in *Love Somebody* and *Gliding*.

LOVE SOMEBODY

LOVE SOMEBODY

On Another Note...

THE ROMANTIC PERIOD (1820–1900)

Delacroix, Eugene (1798–1863), Women of Algiers in Their Room. Scala/ Art Resource, NY.

During the age of Romanticism, composers wanted to make music express inner emotions and feelings. Subjectivity of the heart reigned over objectivity of the head, imagination over form. Subjects focused on love, despair, macabre subjects, death, exotic landscapes, nature, and fantasy. Descriptive titles were frequently used and depicted through the music. Music became an extension of the individual artist's personality and his nationalistic ties as well. This was also the age of the solo performer and the piano was the main keyboard instrument. Many of the Romantic composers were also outstanding solo performers and so took it upon themselves to write music that reflected their own abilities to play very difficult and technically challenging compositions. Composers such as Frédéric Chopin, Franz Liszt, Robert Schumann, Johannes Brahms, and Peter Tchaikovsky are among those who lived during the Romantic period.

TRANSPOSITION

Love Somebody uses the C five-finger position. After you have played this piece as written, play it in the G five-finger position as used in *Whistle Daughter* appearing on page 28. Playing a piece in a different key (a different five-finger pattern) from the original is called **transposition.**

DYNAMIC CHANGES

Crescendo   〈   means to gradually play louder.

Diminuendo (or **decrescendo**)   〉   means to gradually play softer.

Middle C Position

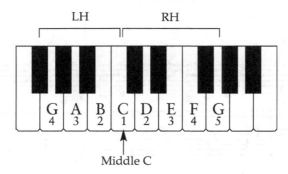

Middle C

1:27

GLIDING

Elyse Mach

Gracefully

Locate the intervals of a third in this piece.

Remember to not look down at the keys when you are playing.

GLIDING

Accompaniment
Gracefully

Arranged by Phillip Keveren

FOURTHS

Fourths skip two white keys.

4th

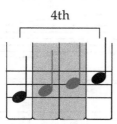

A **fourth** is written from **a line to a space**

4th

OR

from **a space to a line.**

4th

Intervals of a fourth are used in *Chimes Afar.*

DAMPER PEDAL

The **damper pedal,** which is the pedal to the right, is used to sustain tones.

Push the pedal down with the right foot, hold as indicated by the marking, and then release.

pedal   hold   pedal
down   up

Place the ball of your foot on the pedal and keep your heel against the floor.

CHIMES AFAR

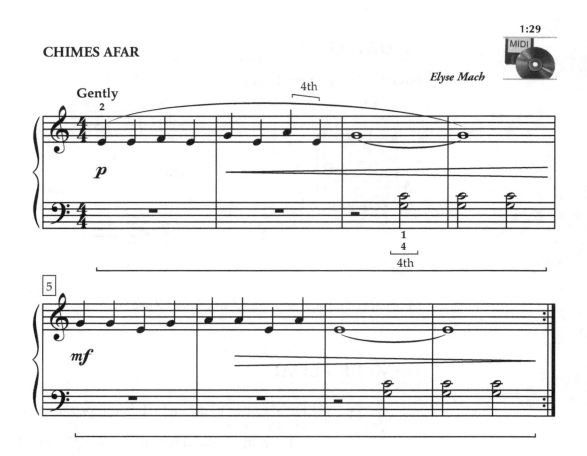

Elyse Mach

CHIMES AFAR

Accompaniment
Gently

Arranged by Ken Iversen

Now play *Chimes Afar* one octave higher in each part with both hands.

FIFTHS

Fifths skip three white keys.

5th

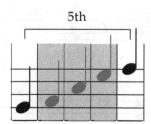

A **fifth** is written from **line to line**

5th

OR
from **space to space.**

5th

Country Tune uses the interval of a fifth in the left-hand accompaniment.

Drone Bass

A **drone bass** is an accompaniment that keeps repeating the harmonic interval of a fifth.

Drone Bass

COUNTRY TUNE

Elyse Mach

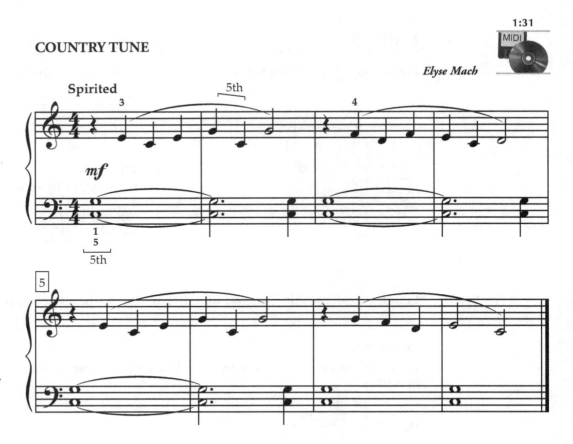

*Now play
Country Tune one
octave lower in the
left-hand part.*

COUNTRY TUNE

Accompaniment
Spirited

Arranged by Phillip Keveren

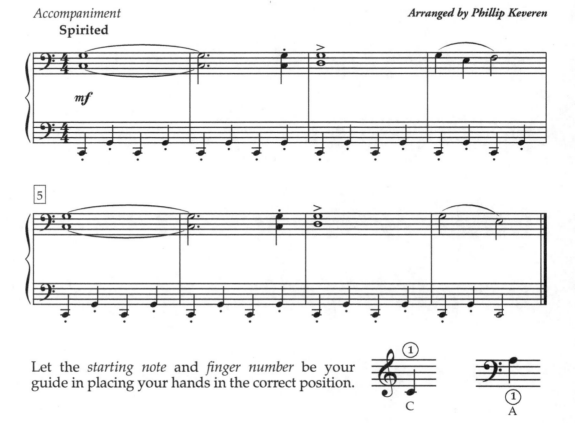

Let the *starting note* and *finger number* be your
guide in placing your hands in the correct position.

SOLO

SWING

Elyse Mach

Easygoing

Remember to not look down at the keys when you are playing.

SWING

Accompaniment
Easygoing

Arranged by Phillip Keveren

UPBEAT AND DOWNBEAT

An **upbeat** begins with a beat other than the first one in the measure. A **down-beat** begins on the first beat. When a piece begins with an upbeat, the missing beats in the first measure will be found at the end of the piece.

Pick out the harmonic intervals that are used in the left-hand part of *When the Saints Go Marching In.*

WHEN THE SAINTS GO MARCHING IN

1:35

Traditional
Arranged by Elyse Mach

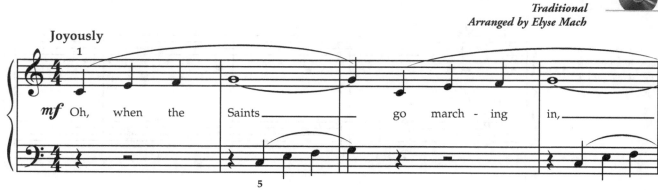

Joyously

mf Oh, when the Saints _____ go march - ing in, _____

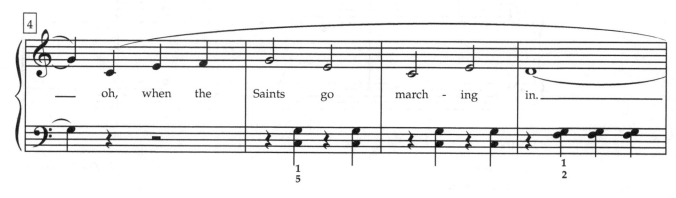

__ oh, when the Saints go march - ing in. _____

__ Oh, how I want to be in that num - ber, _____

__ oh, when the Saints go march - ing in. _____

WHEN THE SAINTS GO MARCHING IN

Traditional
Arranged by Phillip Keveren

Accompaniment
Joyously

ENSEMBLE

MELODY *(Op. 149)*

Antonio Diabelli (1781–1858)
Arranged by Elyse Mach

Piano 1 may be played one octave higher than written.

RHYTHMS TO READ

Tap the various rhythmic patterns that follow. The RH taps the notes with stems going up. The LH taps the notes with stems going down. First tap each hand separately, and then with both hands together.

TRAINING THE EAR

Select one of the interval pairings that your teacher plays. Check the correct response on the blanks provided.

1. a. ___  b. ___

2. a. ___ 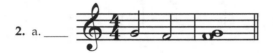 b. ___

3. a. ___  b. ___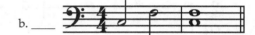

4. a. ___  b. ___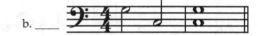

NAME —————————————
DATE —————————————
SCORE —————————————

Short Answer

1. Indicate whether each interval is *harmonic* (by using the letter h) or *melodic* (by using the letter m) and then give the size of the interval.

—— ——   —— ——   —— ——   —— ——   —— ——

Construction

2. Create and write out four measures of rhythm for the following time signatures.

3. Name the following melodic intervals and write the letter names on the blanks below.

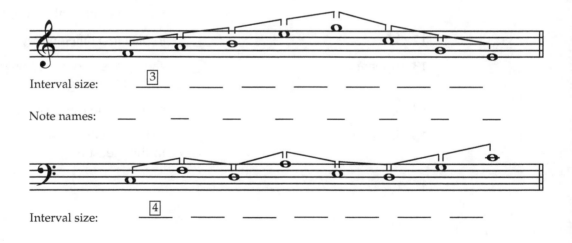

Interval size: 3   ——   ——   ——   ——   ——   ——

Note names: —   —   —   —   —   —   —

Interval size: 4   ——   ——   ——   ——   ——   ——

Note names: —   —   —   —   —   —   —

Matching

Write the numbers from Column A to correspond to the given answers in Column B.

COLUMN A	COLUMN B
1. tie	_____ a musical sentence
2. crescendo	_____ common time
3. diminuendo	_____ the distance between two notes
4. half rest	_____ ▬
5. transposition	_____ to gradually play softer
6. quarter rest	_____ to gradually play louder
7. damper pedal	_____ a curved line connecting notes of the same pitch. The second note is not sounded.
8. drone bass	_____ ▬
9. whole rest	_____ 𝄽
10. leger lines	_____ three beats to a measure with the quarter note receiving the beat
11. phrase	_____ an accompaniment that keeps repeating the harmonic interval of a fifth
12. 𝄴	_____ to play in a different key from the original
13. upbeat	_____ short lines above and below the staff to extend the range
14. ¾	_____ pedal to the right used to sustain tone
15. interval	_____ to begin with a beat other than the first in the measure

4

*M*ore *Reading Basics*

PLAYING IN VARIOUS OCTAVES

Play all the C's that are written on the staves, starting with low C and then moving up eight tones higher (in octaves) each time. Use the fingering given.

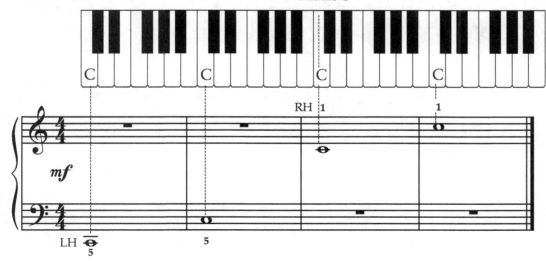

61

Play the following C five-finger position melody in the various octaves going up.

STEPPING UP IN C

1:38

Elyse Mach

STEPPING UP IN C

Accompaniment

Elyse Mach

Now play the following C five-finger position melody in the various octaves going down.

STEPPING DOWN IN C

1:40

Elyse Mach

STEPPING DOWN IN C

Accompaniment

Steadily

Elyse Mach

FERMATA

A **fermata** is used to hold a note longer than its value.

Notice how the melody in *Navajo Chant* is repeated in various octaves.

Focus on the G played by the 4th finger of the right hand melody as it moves from one octave to another.

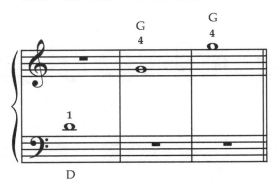

New notation:

Leger lines are used when notes are written higher or lower than the staff.

NAVAJO CHANT

Navajo Song

Andante

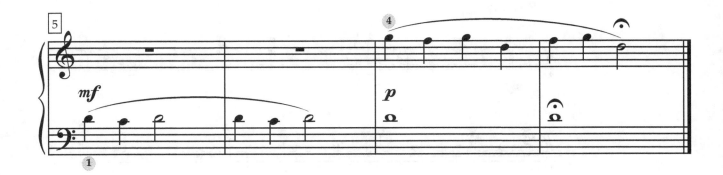

NAVAJO CHANT

Accompaniment   ***Arranged by Phillip Keveren***
Andante

TEMPO MARKINGS

Tempo is the rate of speed or movement. **Tempo markings** indicate how fast or slow the music is to be played.

Allegro	fast; lively
Allegretto	moderately fast
Moderato	moderately
Andante	at a walking pace; moving along
Adagio	slowly

The right hand moves an octave higher using the C five-finger position.

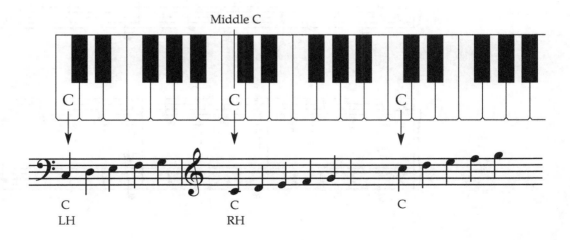

1:44

DIALOGUE

Elyse Mach

DIALOGUE

Accompaniment
Moderato

Arranged by Ken Iversen

FLAT SIGN

♭ A **flat sign** before a note indicates to play the next key to the left. The nearest key may be a black key or a white one.

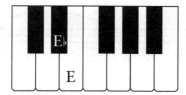

When a flat is used before a note, that note remains flat for the entire measure. The barline cancels out the flat going into the next measure.

The notes remain as E♭   played as E, *not* E♭

1:46

SHORTENIN' BREAD

Folk Tune

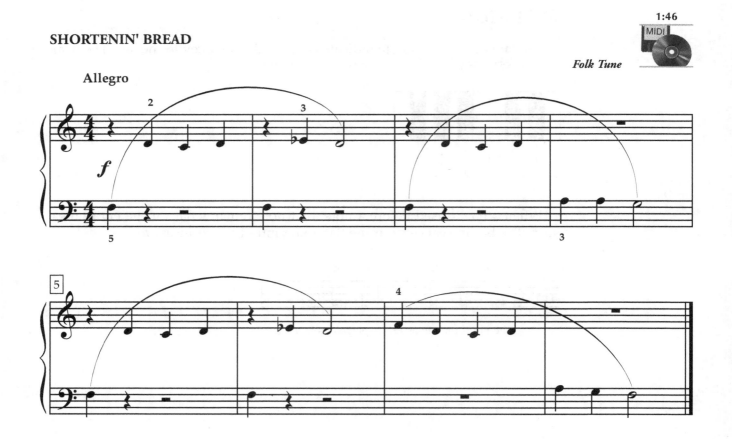

SHORTENIN' BREAD

Folk Tune
Arranged by Ken Iversen

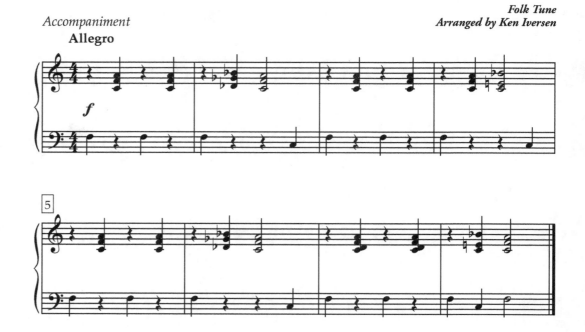

8va

8va ------- | **8va** means to play one octave higher than written when this sign is placed *above* the notes.

SOLO

LATIN MOVES

1:48

Elyse Mach

LATIN MOVES

Accompaniment

Elyse Mach

SHARP SIGN

♯   The **sharp sign** before a note means to play the next key to the right. The nearest key may be a black key or a white one.

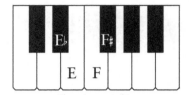

When a sharp is used before a note, that note remains sharp for the entire measure. The barline cancels out the sharp going into the next measure.

The notes remain as F♯   played as F, *not* F♯

8va

8va - - - - - - - ⌐   **8va** means to play one octave lower than written when the sign if placed *under* the notes.

RITARDANDO (RIT.)

A gradual slowing of the tempo.

1:50

ACABA

Elyse Mach

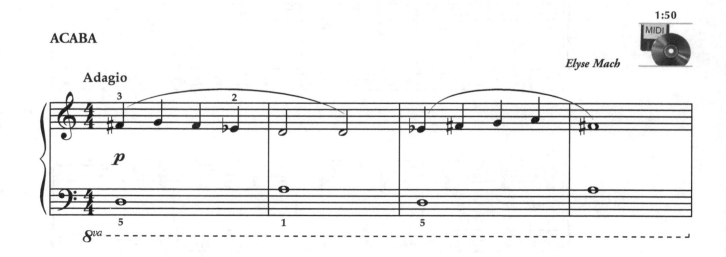

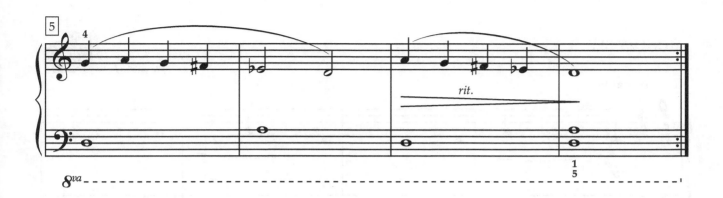

ACABA

Accompaniment   *Arranged by Phillip Keveren*
Adagio

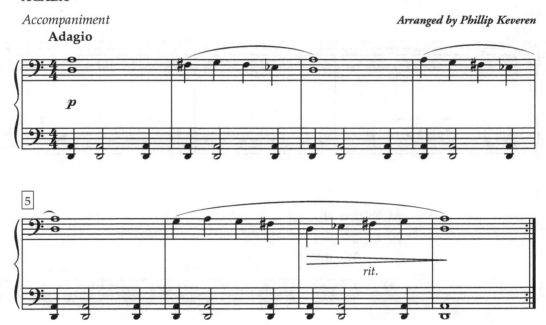

NATURAL SIGN

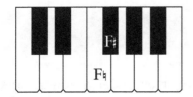 A **natural sign** cancels a sharp or flat. The note always goes back to its natural state.

MONDAY BLUES

Elyse Mach

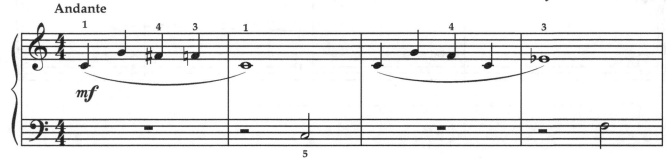

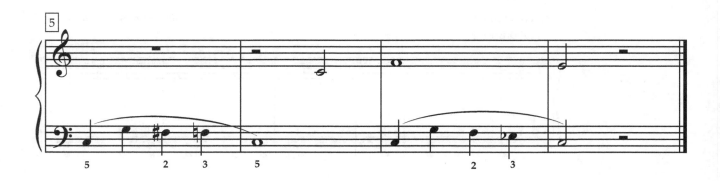

MONDAY BLUES

Accompaniment

Elyse Mach

STACCATO

 Staccato notes have a dot *above* or *below* each note. Play these notes very short and in a detached way.

ACCENT SIGN

 An **accent sign** over or under a note means to play that note louder.

OLE!

Mexican

OLE!

Accompaniment

Arranged by Ken Iversen

SHOESTRING BOOGIE

Elyse Mach

SHOESTRING BOOGIE

Accompaniment
Allegro

Arranged by Phillip Keveren

MORE DYNAMIC MARKINGS

ff   *fortissimo*   very loud
pp   *pianissimo*   very soft

1:58

FANFARE

Elyse Mach

Dal Segno al Fine (*D.S. al Fine*)
Means to repeat from the sign 𝄋 to **Fine.**

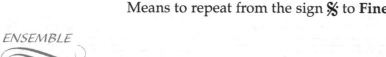

RAZZLE DAZZLE

1:60

Lee Evans

Moderate swing

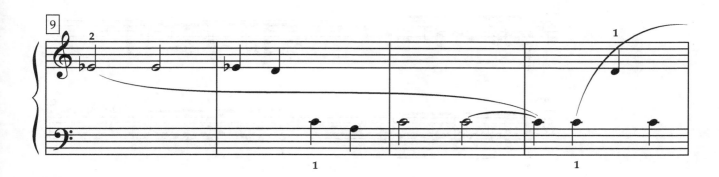

Continued

RAZZLE DAZZLE

Accompaniment
Moderate swing

Lee Evans

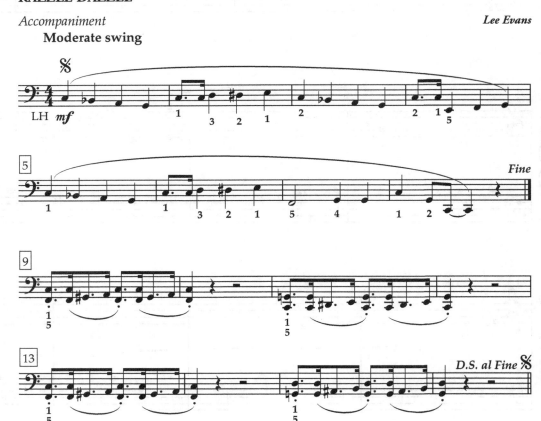

Makoto Ozone *jazz pianist*

On improvising: In improvising, you start learning those musical "clichés" at first, and then as you become more and more familiar with the sound and all, you pick a specific cliché or subject, so to speak, and then develop that subject by changing the melody around, changing the order of the notes, displacing the rhythm, and so on. That's one way to build your improvisational skills.

Source: Courtesy of Makoto Ozone

IMPROVISATION

Open Fifth Improvisation
Improvise various open fifths using them melodically and harmonically in both hands in a style similar to the one provided next.

Explore a wide range of high and low sounds, shifting from one end to the other end of the keyboard. Use some damper pedal (the right pedal) to help blend some of the sounds together. Several measures are given to get you started.

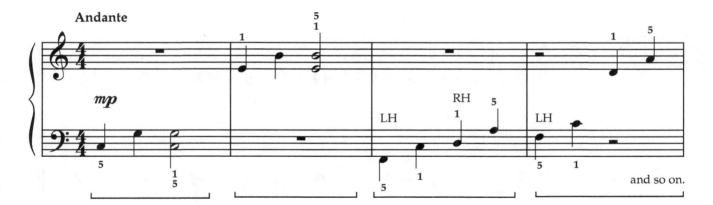

TECHNIQUE

Play the following patterns in various octaves. First play the patterns in the C five-finger position and then transpose to the G five-finger position.

RHYTHMS TO READ

Tap the various rhythmic patterns that follow. The RH taps the notes with the stems going up. The LH taps the notes with stems going down. First tap each hand separately, and then with both hands together.

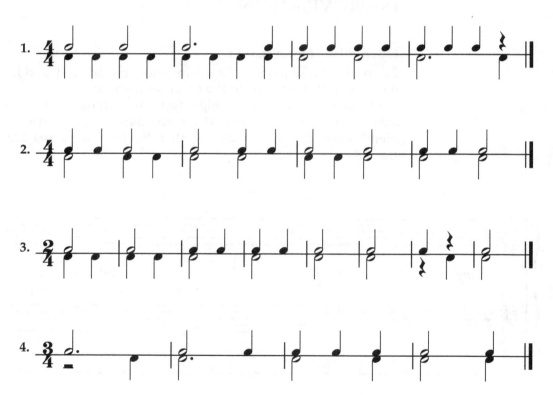

TRAINING THE EAR

Select one of the interval pairings that your teacher plays. Check the correct response on the blanks provided.

1. a. ___    b. ___

2. a. ___    b. ___

3. a. ___    b. ___

4. a. ___    b. ___

Select the correct rhythm that your teacher plays. Check the correct response on the blanks provided.

5. a. ___    b. ___

6. a. ___ 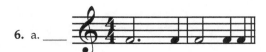   b. ___

7. a. ___    b. ___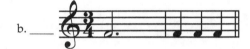

8. a. ___    b. ___

NAME _____

DATE _____

SCORE _____

Short Answer

1. Write the names of the treble clef notes given on the blanks provided.

G

| 1. | 2. | 3. | 4. | 5. | 6. | 7. | 8. | 9. | 10. | 11. | 12. | 13. |

___ ___ ___ ___ ___ ___ ___ ___ ___ ___ ___ ___ ___

2. Write the names of the bass clef notes given on the blanks provided.

F

| 1. | 2. | 3. | 4. | 5. | 6. | 7. | 8. | 9. | 10. | 11. | 12. | 13. |

___ ___ ___ ___ ___ ___ ___ ___ ___ ___ ___ ___ ___

Construction

3. Write the symbol on the blanks next to each term listed.

a. fermata _____

b. natural sign _____

c. flat sign _____

d. sharp sign _____

e. very loud _____

Matching

Write the numbers from Column A to correspond to the given answers in Column B.

COLUMN A	COLUMN B
1. Andante	_____ very loud
2. sharp (♯)	_____ cancels a sharp or flat
3. *8va* ----------	_____ fast and lively
4. *D.S. al Fine*	_____ at a walking pace
5. Allegro	_____ to play in a detached manner
6. flat (♭)	_____ to hold a note longer than its value
7. Adagio	_____ very soft
8. natural (♮)	_____ to begin with a complete measure
9. *ff*	_____ symbol indicating to play the next key to the left
10. *pp*	_____ when appearing above the notes means to play one octave higher than written
11. downbeat	_____ to begin with a beat other than the first
12. upbeat	_____ a symbol indicating to play the next note to the right
13. fermata	_____ a gradual slowing of the tempo
14. ritardando	_____ repeat from the sign 𝄋 to *Fine*.
15. ♩ ♩̇	_____ slowly

Major Five-Finger Patterns and Major Triads

HALF STEP

A **half step** is the distance from one key to the very next key, moving up or down, whether it is a black key or a white one. For example, C to C♯ is a half step, E to E♭ is a half step, and E to F is a half step.

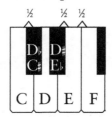

WHOLE STEP

A **whole step** is a combination of two half steps. *Skip one key* and go on to the next one.

For example, E♭ to F is a whole step, B to C♯ is a whole step, and D to E is a whole step.

Practice Strategies

1. Practice building half steps up from the note name given and write the correct answer on the blank lines provided. Use your keyboard to help you.

    1. G _____   6. B _____

    2. E _____   7. G♭ _____

    3. D _____   8. C♯ _____

    4. F♯ _____   9. A _____

    5. D♭ _____   10. E♭ _____

2. Practice building whole steps up from the note name given and write the correct answer on the blank lines provided. Do not repeat or skip any letter names. Use your keyboard to help you.

    1. D _____   6. B _____

    2. F _____   7. G♭ _____

    3. E _____   8. C _____

    4. A♭ _____   9. E♭ _____

    5. F♯ _____   10. B♭ _____

THE MAJOR FIVE-FINGER PATTERN

The **major five-finger pattern** is arranged in the pattern: *whole step, whole step, half step, whole step.*

C Major Five-Finger Pattern

The major five-finger pattern can be constructed on any one of the twelve tones. The first tone of the major five-finger pattern is called the **tonic.** If we build the pattern on C, then C is the tonic.

The major five-finger pattern consists of the first five tones of a major scale (as discussed on page 139).

 PRACTICE DIRECTIONS

1. Practice playing the five-finger patterns given, first starting with the one in C, and then in G, F, and D.
2. Play the patterns with the right hand, then the left one, up and down.
3. Play the patterns with both hands together.

C MAJOR FIVE-FINGER PATTERN

G MAJOR FIVE-FINGER PATTERN

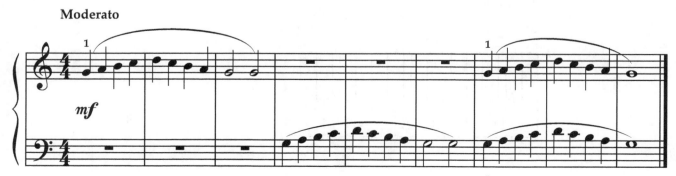

F MAJOR FIVE-FINGER PATTERN

Moderato

D MAJOR FIVE-FINGER PATTERN

Moderato

Practice Strategies

Build and play other major five-finger patterns using the basic whole-step, half-step pattern given. Keyboards are provided so that you can write down the letter names to form the various major five-finger patterns of your choice.

Example:

D Major

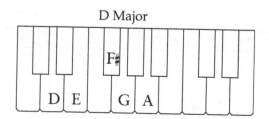

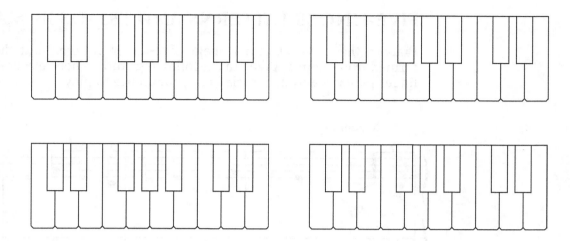

MAJOR TRIADS

A **triad** has three tones:

- the **root (1)**—so called because it is the tone on which the triad is constructed; it is also the note which gives the triad its name.
- the **third (3)**
- the **fifth (5)**

A triad is also called a **chord.**

Major triads are formed by taking the first (root), third, and fifth tones of the major five-finger patterns and sounding them together.

C Major Chord

*RH triads use the
fingering 1–3–5.*

*LH triads use the
fingering 5–3–1.*

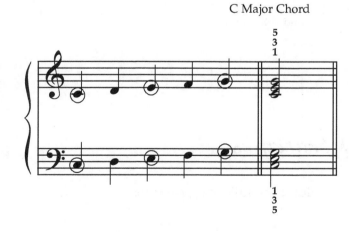

FIVE-FINGER PATTERNS AND TRIADS IN MAJOR

Practice the C, G, D, and F major five-finger patterns and the major triads formed from them as given in the following study. Then select other major five-finger patterns and major triads of your choice to play.

EIGHTH NOTES

Two **eighth notes** are equal to one quarter note and should be played *evenly*. When two eighth notes are paired together, a **beam** is used.

Practice counting the eighth notes like this:

$$\frac{4}{4}$$

```
1    &    2    &    3    &
(1   and  2    and  3    and
```

Practice Strategies

Clap and count aloud the following rhythms.

1. $\frac{4}{4}$

count: 1   &   2   &   3   &   4   &   1   &   2   &   3   &   4   &

Source: Library of Congress, Prints & Photographs Division, reproduction number, LC-D420-2392.

On Another Note...

JOHANN SEBASTIAN BACH

Johann Sebastian Bach (1685–1750) was born into a musical family and several of his sons went on to become composers. Born in the small town of Eisenach, Bach lived in Germany all of his life working in various posts as violinist, organist, and musical director. He wrote instrumental music for court functions and choral music for the services in the Lutheran churches at Leipzig—where he directed the choir at St. Thomas's Church and taught singing and Latin in the church's school. In the 1730s, Bach even provided music—his own or the music of other contemporary composers—for the weekly concerts at Zimmermann's Coffee House and Gardens. During his life, Bach received recognition for his exceptional talents as an organist and improviser. The composer of hundreds of compositions in most all the forms prevalent in the late Baroque, except for opera, he is considered by many to be the greatest composer of the Baroque period. Bach was married twice and had twenty children, of whom only ten survived infancy. To this day, the four-hundred-year-old Bach-Haus Museum in Eisenach stands on the same location as the original Bach family house, and it is furnished with the furniture and objects from Bach's time.

CASEY JONES *(C Major Five-Finger Pattern)*

1:61
MIDI

American

CASEY JONES

Accompaniment

Arranged by Elyse Mach

1:63

MUSETTE *(G Major Five-Finger Pattern)*

Johann Sebastian Bach (1685–1750)
Arranged by Elyse Mach

MUSETTE

Accompaniment

Arranged by Ken Iversen

SHALL WE GATHER AT THE RIVER *(D Major Five-Finger Pattern)*

Words and Music by
Robert Lowry (1826–1899)

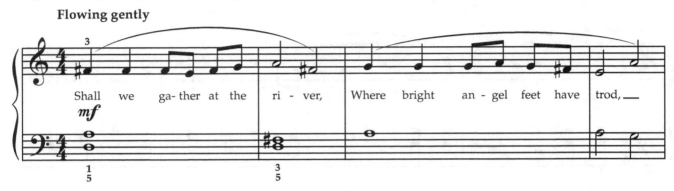

Shall we ga-ther at the ri - ver, Where bright an - gel feet have trod, ___

With its cry-stal tide for - e - ver Flow-ing by the ___ throne of ___ God.

rit.

SHALL WE GATHER AT THE RIVER

Accompaniment

Flowing gently

Arranged by Elyse Mach

rit.

SONG OF PRAISE *(F Major Five-Finger Pattern)*

Adapted Hymn

SONG OF PRAISE

Accompaniment

Arranged by Phillip Keveren

FRENCH FOLK SONG

French
Arranged by Elyse Mach

Dave Brubeck *jazz pianist*

On improvising: What young musicians should learn is improvisation. During the time of Bach, Mozart, and Beethoven, musicians were expected to improvise. . . . Those who attended church in Leipzig were almost certain that Bach would improvise during the Sunday service, and during the Classical period, people would hire Mozart to come and play, in the same way that we listen to jazz musicians today.

IMPROVISATION

Improvise C major five-finger melodies to the repeated left-hand accompaniment of open fifths (called a **drone bass accompaniment** as discussed earlier on page 51).

The drone bass accompaniment can be formed using other major five-finger patterns by taking the first and fifth tones in the five-finger pattern and playing them together on the first beat of each measure.

IMPROVISATION *C Major Five-Finger Melodies/Drone Bass Accompaniment*

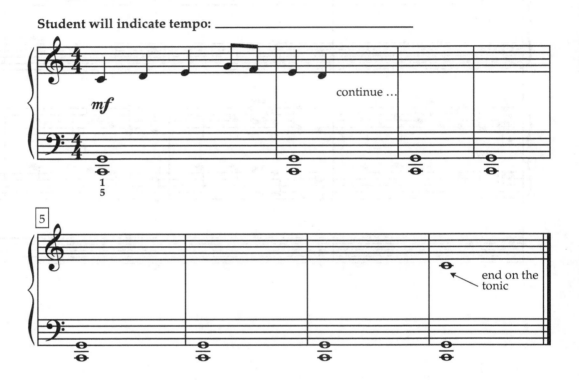

TECHNIQUE

The Chromatic Scale

The **chromatic scale** uses only half steps. It can begin on any tone and uses all of the twelve tones.

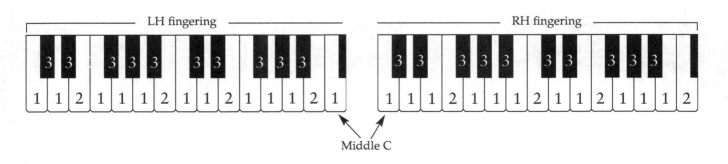

Preparatory Chromatic Scale Study

1. Use finger 3 on each black key. Practice going up and down the black keys with **only** finger 3 of the RH and then finger 3 of the LH.

2. Practice going up and down the white keys with finger 1 (the thumb) on each white key except the pair of white keys (B–C and E–F), where 2-1 will be used in the LH and 1-2 will be used in the right hand.

3. Play the chromatic scale using the fingering chart given on the keyboard, first with hands separately, and then with both hands together.

RHYTHMS TO READ

Tap the various rhythmic patterns that follow. The RH taps the notes with the stems going up. The LH taps the notes with stems going down. First tap each hand separately, and then with both hands together.

TRAINING THE EAR

Select one of the melodic patterns that your teacher plays. Check the correct response on the blanks provided.

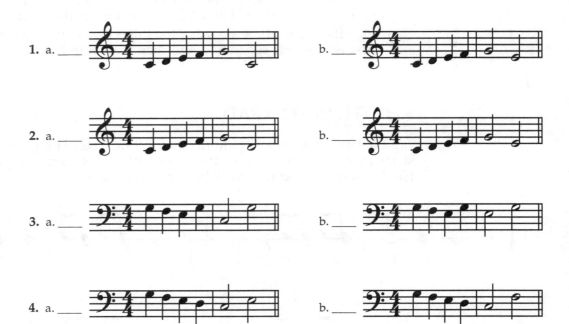

6

Minor Five–Finger Patterns and Minor Triads

THE MINOR FIVE-FINGER PATTERN

The **minor five-finger pattern** is arranged in the pattern: *whole step, half step, whole step, whole step.*

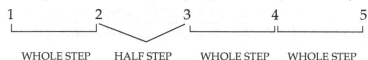

| 1 | | 2 | | 3 | | 4 | | 5 |

WHOLE STEP   HALF STEP   WHOLE STEP   WHOLE STEP

C Minor Five-Finger Pattern

An easy way to play the minor five-finger pattern is to begin with the major five-finger pattern and to lower the third (or middle note) a half step.

101

Frédéric Chopin *Romantic period composer/pianist/teacher*
from the book **Chopin: Pianist and Teacher**

Find the right position for the hand by placing your fingers on the keys, E,
F♯, G♯, A♯, B: the long fingers occupy the high keys, and the short fingers
the low keys. Place the fingers occupying the high keys all on one level and
do the same for those occupying the white keys, to make the leverage
equal; this will curve the hand giving it the necessary suppleness that it
could not have if the fingers were straight. A supple hand: the wrist, the
forearm, the arm, everything will follow the hand in the right order.

*Source: Library of Congress,
Prints and Photographs Divi-
sion, reproduction number
LC-US Z62-110983*

NEW TIME SIGNATURE: $\frac{2}{4}$

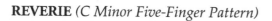

$\frac{2}{4}$ 2 beats to the measure.

the quarter note (♩) receives the beat.

Play other five-finger melodies such as *Love Somebody* (page 46) and *Ode to Joy*
(page 26) in minor by lowering the third (or middle note) a half step.

REVERIE (*C Minor Five-Finger Pattern*)

French

1:72

CHICKALILEEO *(G Minor Five-Finger Pattern)*

Traditional
Arranged by Elyse Mach

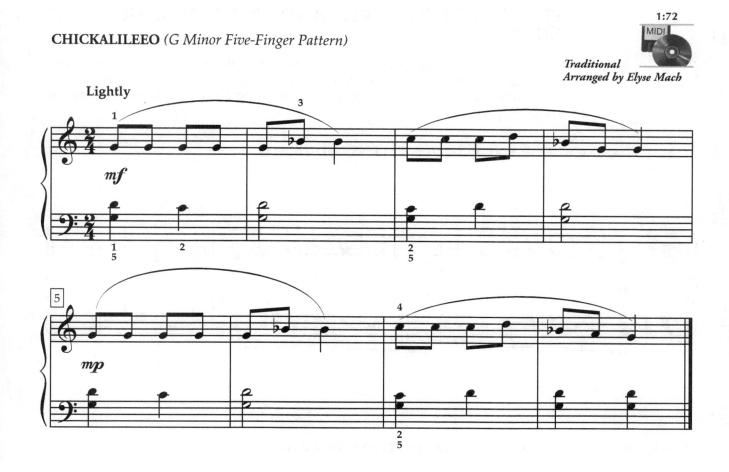

MINOR TRIADS

Minor triads are formed by taking the first (root), third, and fifth tones of the minor five-finger pattern and sounding them together.

C Minor Chord

RH triads use the fingering 1–3–5.

LH triads use the fingering 5–3–1.

FIVE-FINGER PATTERNS AND TRIADS IN MAJOR AND MINOR

Practice the following study that uses major and minor five-finger patterns and the major and minor triads formed from them in C, G, F, and D. Then select other major and minor five-finger patterns along with their major and minor triads to play.

C MAJOR AND C MINOR FIVE-FINGER PATTERNS AND TRIADS

G MAJOR AND G MINOR FIVE-FINGER PATTERNS AND TRIADS

---

*Symbol for C major → C
**Symbol for C minor → Cm

F MAJOR AND F MINOR FIVE-FINGER PATTERNS AND TRIADS

D MAJOR AND D MINOR FIVE-FINGER PATTERNS AND TRIADS

A TEMPO

A tempo means to return to the original tempo.

SOLO

AARON'S SONG

Aaron Peirick

*The damper pedal is optional.

AARON'S SONG

Accompaniment

Elyse Mach

Play an octave higher than written.

ENSEMBLE

SPRING *from* The Four Seasons

Antonio Vivaldi (1678–1741)
Arranged by Ken Iversen

1:76

Continued

NAME ——————————

DATE ——————————

SCORE ——————————

Short Answer

1. Identify the quality (major or minor) of the triads below. Use the uppercase letter to signify major (i.e., D for D major) and the uppercase letter followed by a small m to signify minor (i.e., Dm for D minor).

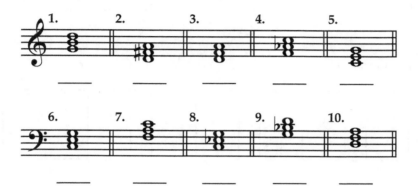

Construction

2. Finish the following rhythm patterns in the meter signatures given using only *one* note to complete each measure.

3. Build each of the major and minor five-finger patterns on the keyboards provided. Be sure to use five different letter names for each one of the five-finger patterns that you build.

1. C major

2. C minor

3. G major

4. G minor

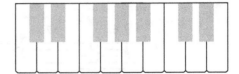

5. F major

6. F minor

7. D major

8. D minor

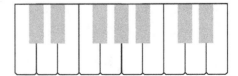

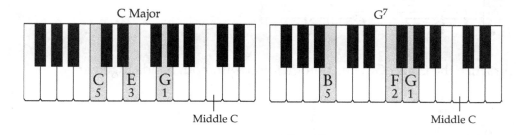
Harmonizing Melodies

USING THE C MAJOR AND G⁷ CHORDS

Chords are frequently used to form the accompaniment for melodies. The C major and G^7 chords are used often as an accompaniment.

Many printed versions of folk tunes and popular songs do not include any accompaniment; instead, chords are identified merely by letter names (referred to as chord symbols).

C Major

C
5

E
3

G
1

Middle C

G^7

B
5

F
2

G
1

Middle C

Chord Symbols:

C

1
3
5

G^7

1
2
5

An easy way to move from the C chord to the G⁷ using the left hand is to remember the following steps:

1. The *top* note remains the *same.* **The 1st finger plays the note G in both of the chords.**

2. The *middle* note moves *up a half step.* **The 2nd finger plays the note F in the G⁷ chord.**

3. The *bottom* note moves *down a half step.* **The 5th finger moves out of the C position to play the note B in the G⁷ chord.**

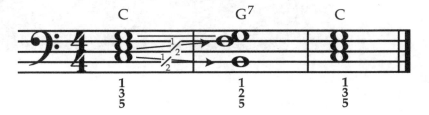

Practice Strategies

1. A **chord progression** consists of two or more chords that are played consecutively when harmonizing a melody. Practice playing the C and G⁷ chord progression with the left hand until you can play it with ease.

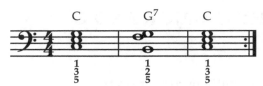

2. Practice the C and G⁷ chord progression with the right hand. **Be sure to use the correct right hand fingerings as given.**

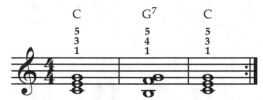

3. Practice the C and G⁷ chord progression with both hands together.

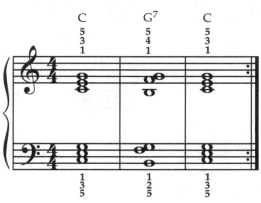

SOLO

1:77

MARY ANN

Calypso Song

In measures 6 and 14 the right hand thumb moves out of the C position to play the melody note of B.

*Gently roll the chords
bottom to top.*

BELLS OF LONDON

Traditional

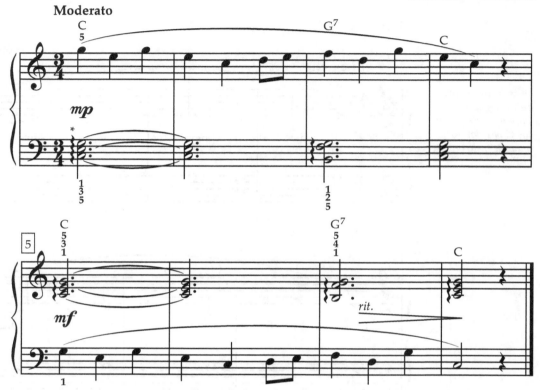

GERMAN FOLK SONG

German

USING THE F MAJOR CHORD

The F major chord is used often along with the C and G^7 chords in accompaniments to melodies. For more ease in playing the change of chords in the accompaniment, the F chord is used in the following arrangement which appears below:

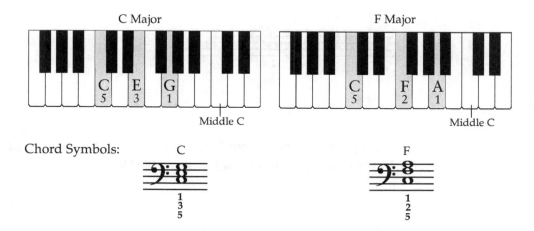

An easy way to move from the C chord to the F chord using the left hand is to remember the following steps:

1. The *top* note moves *up a whole step.* **The 1st finger moves out of the C position to play the note A in the F major chord.**

2. The *middle* note moves *up a half step.* **The 2nd finger plays the note F in the F major chord.**

3. The *bottom* note remains *the same.* **The 5th finger plays the note C in both of the chords.**

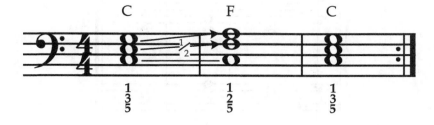

Practice Strategies

1. Practice playing the C and F chord progression with the left hand until you can play it with ease.

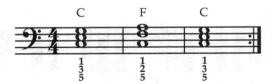

2. Practice the C and F chord progression with the right hand. **Be sure to use the correct right hand fingerings as given.**

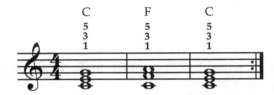

3. Practice the C and F chord progression with both hands together.

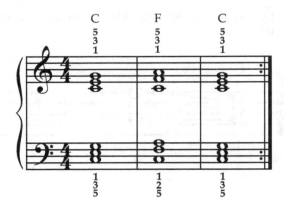

PLAYING THE C MAJOR, F MAJOR, AND G⁷ CHORD PROGRESSION

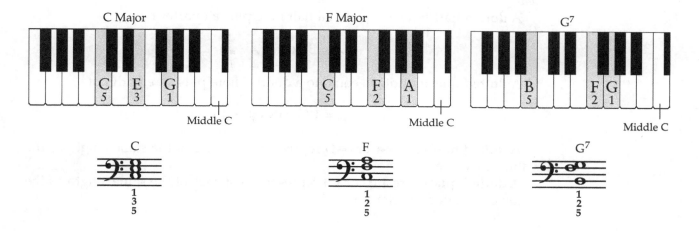

The C, F, and G⁷ chords are constructed on the first, fourth, and fifth tones of the C major scale. They are the strongest and most important chords and are referred to as the **primary chords.**

Practice Strategies

Practice playing the C, F, and G⁷ chord progression with each hand separately, and then with both hands together. **Be sure to use the correct fingerings as given for both hands.**

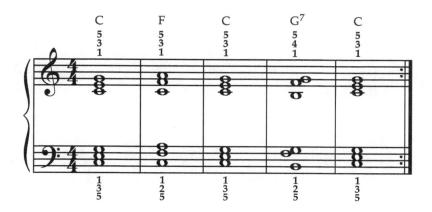

DOTTED QUARTER NOTES

A **dot** placed after a note indicates that the note's value is to be increased by *one half.*

A **dotted half note** is equal to a half note plus a quarter note.

$$\text{♩.} = 3 \text{ beats} \left(\underset{2}{\text{♩}} + \underset{1}{\text{♩}} \right)$$

A **dotted quarter note** is equal to a quarter note plus an eighth note.

$$\text{♩.} = 1\frac{1}{2} \text{ beats} \left(\underset{1}{\text{♩}} + \underset{\frac{1}{2}}{\text{♪}} \right)$$

A **dotted half rest** (▬ or ▬𝄽) represents a silence of the same length as the value of a dotted half note.

A **dotted quarter rest** (𝄽· or 𝄽𝄾) represents a silence of the same length as the value of a dotted quarter note.

Practice Strategies

Clap or tap the following rhythm patterns which use dotted half and dotted quarter note patterns.

1.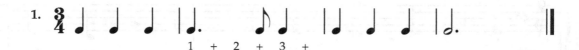

2.

3.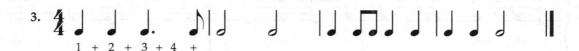

SOLO

JINGLE BELLS

J. S. Pierpont (1822–1893)

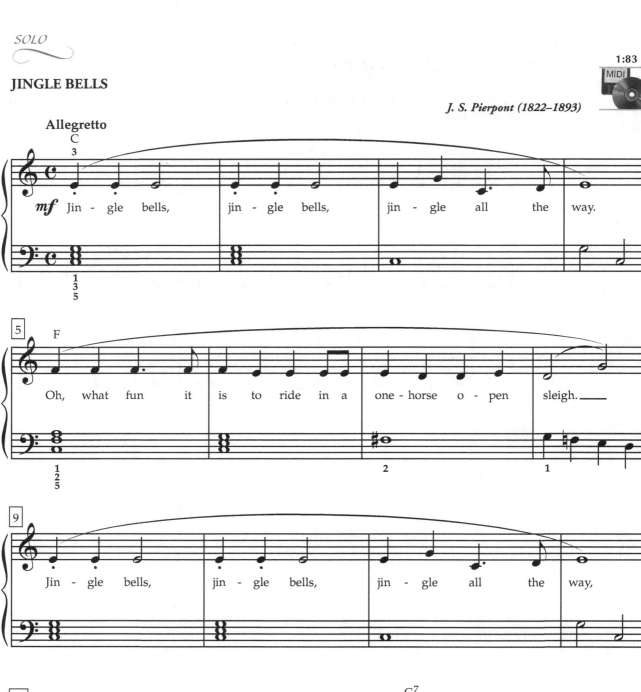

JINGLE BELLS

J. S. Pierpont (1822–1893)
Arranged by Phillip Keveren

Accompaniment
Allegretto

ALLA BREVE (¢)

Alla breve is a time signature that indicates **cut time** (**2/2**). Count **one** beat for each half note.

KUM BA YAH

Traditional

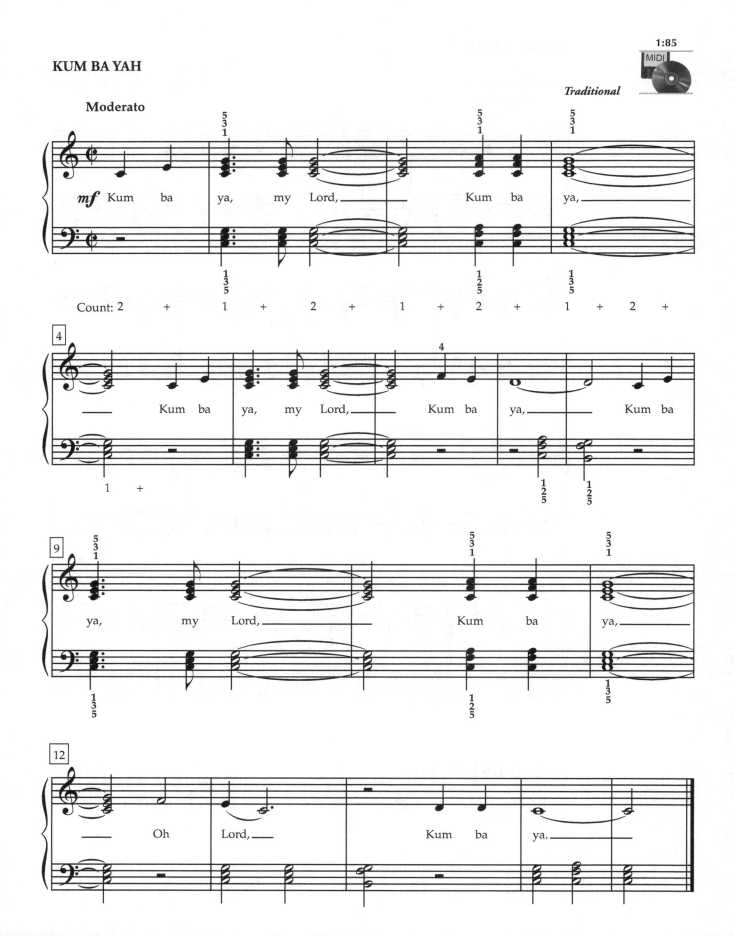

KUM BA YAH

Traditional
Arranged by Ken Iversen

Accompaniment
Moderato

CHANGING FIVE-FINGER POSITIONS

Changing five-finger positions involves moving from one five-finger position to another. The entire hand will shift to a new position.

Perpetual Rock begins in the five-finger pattern of D, shifts to the five-finger pattern of C, and then returns to the original pattern of D. Practice this hand-position shift before playing *Perpetual Rock.*

PERPETUAL ROCK

Elyse Mach

Time-Clock Blues begins in the five-finger pattern of C, shifts to the five-finger pattern of F, then to the five-finger pattern of G, and then returns to the original pattern of C.

Practice this hand-position shift before playing *Time-Clock Blues*. Remember to look ahead of the notes you are playing to prepare for the hand-position changes.

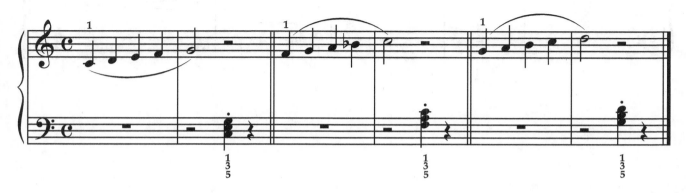

SOLO

TIME-CLOCK BLUES

Elyse Mach

THE DAMPER PEDAL

As discussed in Unit 3 (p. 49), the right pedal is called the **damper pedal.** It is used to add more resonance to the tone and to connect and sustain tones that require legato playing.

Direct Pedaling

Push the pedal down with the right foot, hold as indicated by the marking, and then release. Remember to keep your heel against the floor.

Practice Strategies

Using direct pedaling, practice playing the following pedal study.

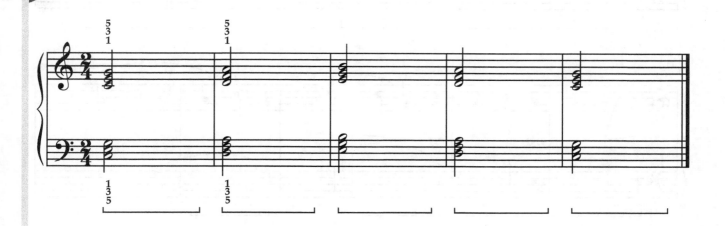

SOLO

MOONLIT SEA

1:91

Phillip Keveren

Scottish Highlands uses direct pedaling. Practice lifting the hands at the end of each phrase along with the pedal lifts.

SOLO

SCOTTISH HIGHLANDS

1:93
MIDI

Elyse Mach

CANON

Johann Pachelbel (1653–1706)
Arranged by Ken Iversen

1:95

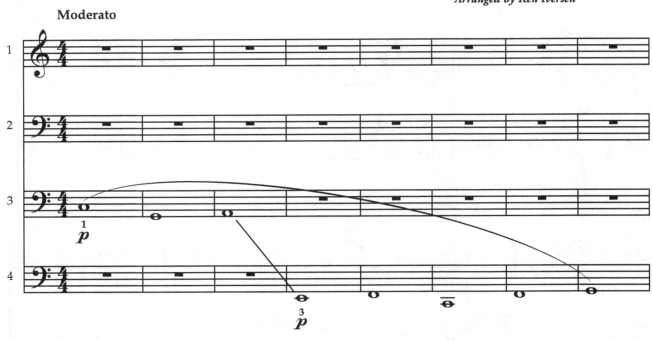

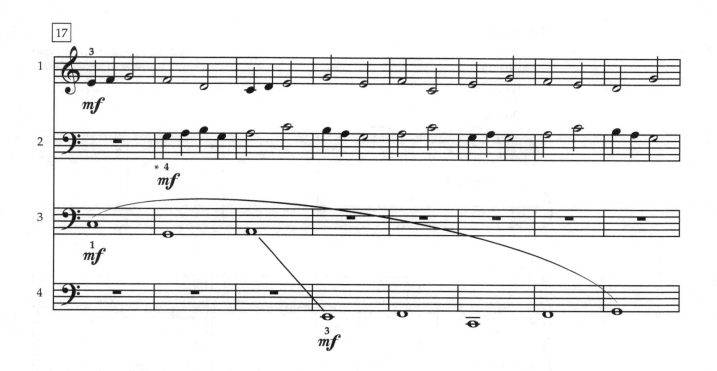

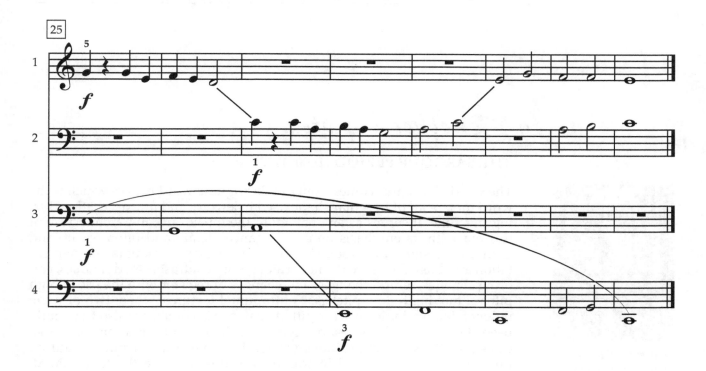

*Put finger 4 on G.

CANON

Johann Pachelbel (1653–1706)
Arranged by Ken Iversen

Accompaniment

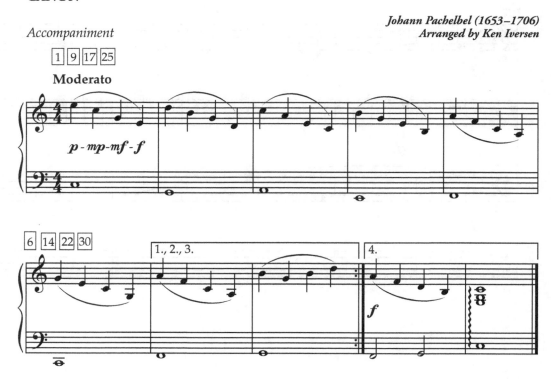

O*n* A*nother* N*ote...*

THE BAROQUE PERIOD (1600–1750)

Source: Bernini, Gian Lorenzo (1598–1680). Ecstasy of St. Theresa. Scala/Art Resource, NY.

The word "Baroque" comes from the Portuguese word *barroco* which is the word for a pearl of irregular shape used in jewelry and fine decoration during this time. It serves as an analogy to the music, art, and architecture of this era with its emphasis on extravagance, detail, and often ornate and grandiose designs. In Baroque keyboard music, large amounts of ornamentation and busy detail are the norm along with contrasts—of dynamics, coloring changes, tempo changes, and changes of register with the use of high pitches moving to low pitches. Contrapuntal textures, where two or more independent melodic lines are pitted against each other, are also frequently used. Preludes and fugues, dance suites, theme and variations, and toccatas are styles of compositions written for keyboard instruments during this period. The keyboard instruments of this time are the harpsichord, clavichord, and the organ. Johann Sebastian Bach, George Frederick Handel, Antonio Vivaldi, and Domenico Scarlatti are representative composers of the period.

HARMONIZING A LEAD-LINE MELODY

Many printed versions of folk tunes and popular songs do not include any accompaniment; instead, chords are identified merely by letter names over a melody that is notated on a single staff. This kind of music notation is referred to as a **lead line.**

The pianist must be able to play the chords that are indicated or play an accompaniment style based on the chord letter-name symbols given in the music.

The following melodies use letter-name symbols that are played with the left hand. Follow the block-chord accompaniment pattern illustrated in the first three measures as you harmonize the melody of the following song.

Measures not having chord symbols displayed will repeat the chord indicated in the previous measure.

RHYTHMS TO READ

Tap the various rhythmic patterns that follow. The RH taps the notes with the stems going up. The LH taps the notes with the stems going down. First tap each hand separately, and then with both hands together.

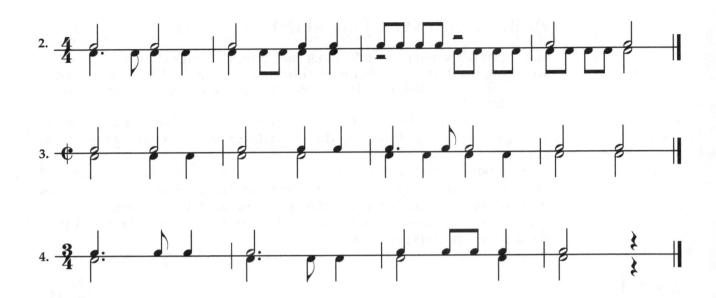

TRAINING THE EAR

1. Select one of the chord groupings that your teacher plays. The chords played will be C, F, and G^7. Check the correct response on the blanks provided.

2. Select the correct rhythmic example that will be played by your teacher. Check the correct response on the blanks provided.

NAME _____
DATE _____
SCORE _____

Short Answer

1. Identify the chords that are given. The C, F, and G^7 chords will be used. Place your answers on the blanks provided.

___   ___   ___   ___   ___   ___

2. Write the correct fingering to the left of each chord.

Construction

3. Write the letter names for each of the chords indicated. The first letter name of the chord is given to get you started.

C   _C_   ____   ____

F   _C_   ____   ____

G^7 _B_   ____   ____

4. Complete each measure of the four measures of rhythm for the following time signatures. Be sure to include some examples of eighth notes in the measure (measure 3) you are asked to create.

Matching

Write the numbers from Column A to correspond to the given answers in Column B.

COLUMN A	COLUMN B
1. ₵	_____ return to the original tempo
2. triad	_____ cut time
3. whole step	_____ a line that joins two eighth notes
4. major five-finger pattern	_____ first tone of a five-finger pattern
5. a tempo	_____ a root, third, and fifth
6. minor five-finger pattern	_____ a combination of two half steps
7. chromatic scale	_____ ws ws hs ws
8. tonic	_____ ws hs ws ws
9. $\frac{2}{4}$	_____ built on half steps only
10. beam	_____ two quarter notes to the measure with the ♩ receiving the beat

The Major Scale / Reading in C Major

THE MAJOR SCALE

Most melodies and chords are based on some kind of scale system. A **scale** (from the Italian word *scala*, ladder) is a step-by-step series of tones in a specific pattern. For example, the **major scale** has eight tones with half steps between tones **3–4** and **7–8,** and whole steps between all of the other tones.

THE C MAJOR SCALE

The **C major scale** has half steps between E–F and B–C. All the other tones have whole steps between them.

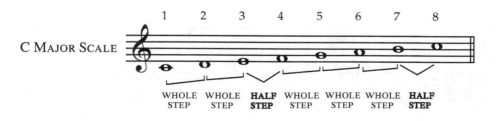

C MAJOR SCALE

139

THE MAJOR SCALE IN TETRACHORD POSITION

Any major scale can be divided into two equal parts, each having four notes. These four-note patterns are called **tetrachords,** and each tetrachord has the pattern:

whole step, whole step, half step.

THE C MAJOR SCALE IN TETRACHORD POSITION

A $\boxed{\text{whole step}}$ joins the two tetrachords.

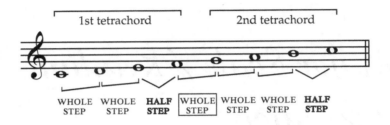

An easy way to start playing the major scales is by using four fingers (no thumbs) in each hand to build the two tetrachords.

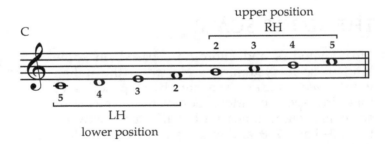

Practice Strategies

Practice playing the following warm-up scale preparation exercises. Note that *crossing over* and *crossing under fingering* are used in playing these exercises.

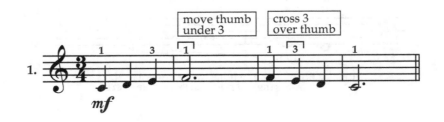

PLAYING THE C MAJOR SCALE IN CONTRARY MOTION

1. Play with hands separately, then with hands together.
2. Use minimal movement in the hands and wrists. No twisting or turning of the wrists.
3. Work for an even and smooth legato from one note to the next.
4. Slightly tilt the hand in the direction you are playing.
5. Memorize the fingering.
6. Notice that the same fingers are used in both hands when playing the C major scale in contrary motion.

C MAJOR SCALE—CONTRARY MOTION

PLAYING THE C MAJOR SCALE IN PARALLEL MOTION

1. Play with hands separately, then with hands together.
2. Use the same suggestions for playing the C major scale in parallel motion as given for playing the C major scale in contrary motion.
3. Memorize the fingering.
4. The places where both hands use the same finger numbers are bracketed to help you learn the correct fingerings more quickly.

C MAJOR SCALE—PARALLEL MOTION

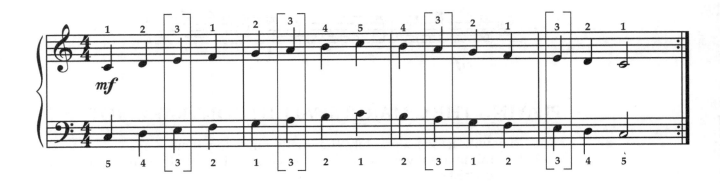

Play these scale study pieces, always working for even and smoothly connected tones.

SCALE STUDY NO. 1

Elyse Mach

SCALE STUDY NO. 2

Elyse Mach

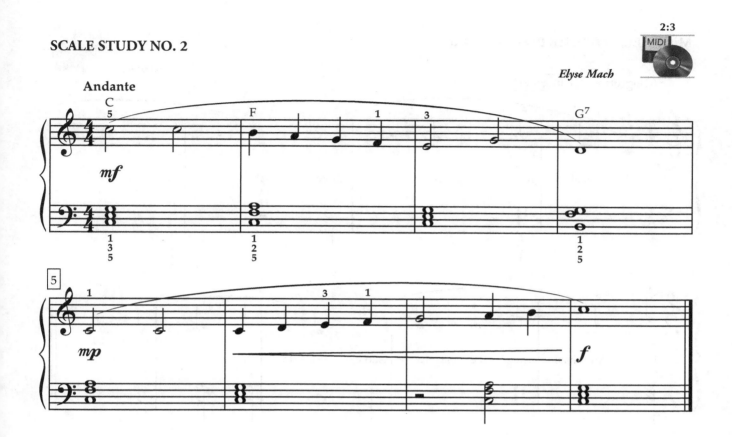

Michael, Row the Boat Ashore extends the 2nd finger of the right hand to play the note E which is called a **finger extension**.

Review Warm-Up

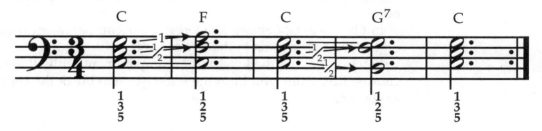

MICHAEL, ROW THE BOAT ASHORE

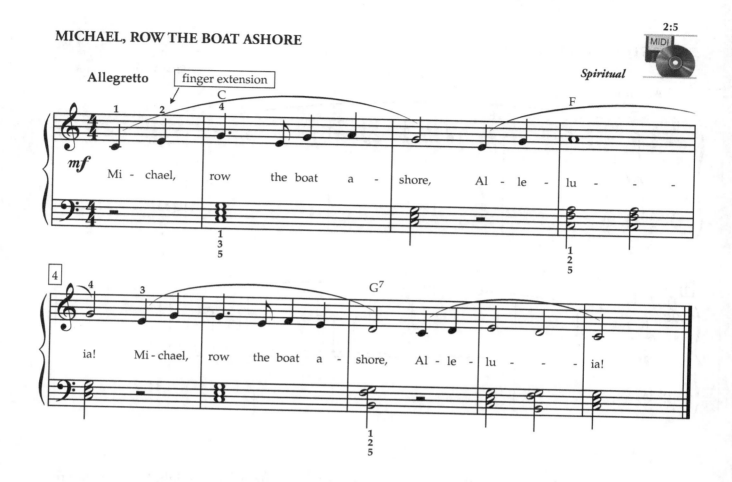

PLAYING AN ARPEGGIO ACCOMPANIMENT PATTERN

An **arpeggio** is a chord in which every note is played separately, one after the other.

In *On Top of Old Smoky*, the left-hand accompaniment uses arpeggios based on C, F, and G^7 chords in the key of C major.

Practice playing the left-hand accompaniment with all tones together (block chords) first while you hum the melody. Then break the chords into arpeggios as shown.

Finger substitution is used in measure 8, where the 2nd finger is replaced on G by the 5th finger.

ON TOP OF OLD SMOKY

2:7

Traditional

TERNARY FORM

Form refers to the architecture or structure of the music. **Ternary form** has three sections and is referred to as **three-part** or **ABA form.**

CLASSIC TWIST

Elyse Mach

Moderato

A (and return to A)

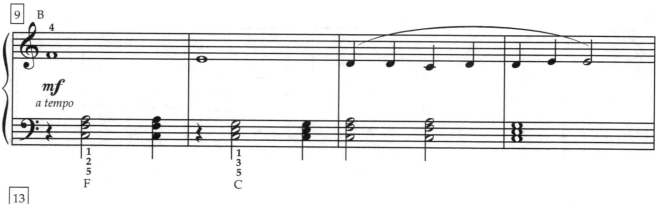

CLASSIC TWIST

Accompaniment
Moderato

Arranged by Phillip Keveren

INTERVALS OF SIXTH, SEVENTH, AND EIGHTH (OCTAVES)

Intervals of a sixth, seventh, and eighth (octave) require an expansion or stretch of the hands.

Practice Strategies

Practice playing the following intervals, which are given both melodically and harmonically in the key of C. First practice hands separately, and then with both hands together.

SIXTHS

An interval of a **sixth** skips four white keys.

On a staff, a **sixth** is written from **line to space**

OR

from **space to line**.

BINARY FORM

Binary form has two sections and is referred to as **two-part** or **AB form.**

SIXTH DEGREE

Elyse Mach

SEVENTHS

An interval of a **seventh** skips five white keys.

On a staff, a **seventh** is written from **line to line**

OR

from **space to space**.

EIGHTHS (OCTAVES)

An interval of an **eighth** (octave) skips six white keys.

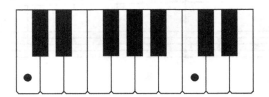

On a staff, an **eighth (octave)** is written from **a line to a space**

OR

from **a space to a line**.

URUBAMBA MAJESTY

Elyse Mach

Arthur Rubinstein *concert pianist, from his biography* **My Many Years**

I cannot tell you how much I love to play for people . . . sometimes when I sit down to practice and there is no one else in the room, I have to stifle my impulse to ring for the elevator man and offer him money to come in and hear me.

HARMONIZING A LEAD-LINE MELODY

Harmonize the lead-line melody with a block-chord accompaniment using the chords indicated by the letter-name symbols.

BEAUTIFUL BROWN EYES

Traditional

Harmonize the melody using an arpeggio accompaniment pattern as illustrated in the first few measures.

BEAUTIFUL BROWN EYES

Traditional

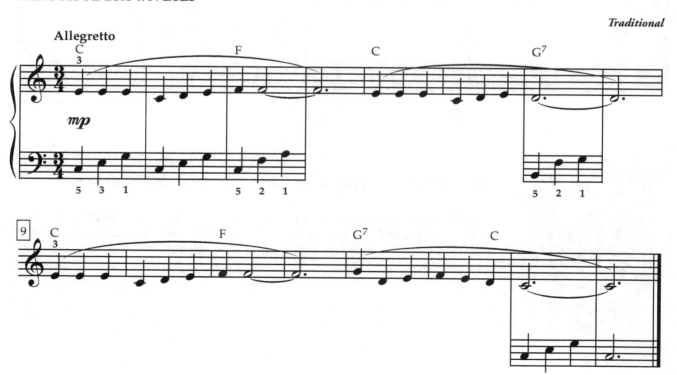

TRAINING THE EAR

Select one of the interval pairings that your teacher plays. The intervals played will be sixths, sevenths, or eighths (octaves). Check the correct response on the blanks provided.

1. a. _____    b. _____

2. a. _____    b. _____

3. a. _____    b. _____

4. a. _____ 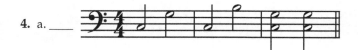   b. _____

5. a. _____    b. _____

UNIT 8   WORKSHEET REVIEW

NAME _____

DATE _____

SCORE _____

Short Answer

1. Identify the kinds of fingering used in the examples given below. The choices are:

    a. extended fingering
    b. contracted fingering
    c. fingering substitution
    d. crossing over and/or under

Place the corresponding letter on the blanks provided under each example.

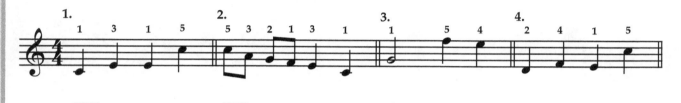

2. Name the following intervals given. Indicate whether each interval is *harmonic* (h) or *melodic* (m) and then give the size of the interval.

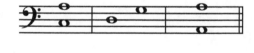

Construction

3. Build harmonic intervals *up* from the notes given. Then write the letter names on the blanks provided.

    3rd   5th   7th   4th   6th   8th

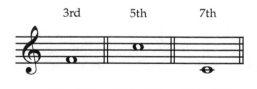

3. Build the C major scale and then indicate the whole step (ws)–half step (hs) patterns used in building the scale. Two of the scale tones are given to get you started. Put the letter names for the C major scale on the blanks provided and place ws or hs in the circles given.

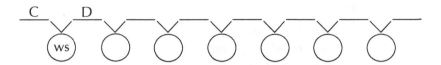

Reading in G Major

THE G MAJOR SCALE

The **G major scale** has eight tones with half steps between B–C and F♯–G, and with whole steps between all of the other tones. The F♯ is used to preserve the pattern of whole steps and half steps of the G major scale.

When a piece is based on the G major scale, it is written in the **key** of G major.

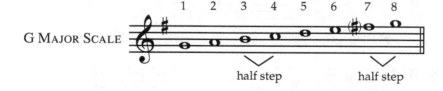

The **key signature** is the F♯ located at the beginning of each staff. It indicates that every F in the key of G major will be played as F♯ throughout the piece.

THE G MAJOR SCALE IN TETRACHORD POSITION

The left hand will start on G to build the first four-note tetrachord pattern and the right hand will start on D to build the second four-note tetrachord. Remember that a whole step joins the two tetrachords.

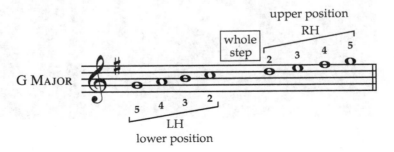

Practice Strategies

Practice playing the following warm-up scale preparation exercises.

PLAYING THE G MAJOR SCALE IN CONTRARY MOTION

1. Play with hands separately, then with hands together.
2. Use minimal movement in the hands and wrists. No twisting or turning of the wrists.
3. Work for an even and smooth legato from one note to the next.
4. Slightly tilt the hand in the direction you are playing.
5. Memorize the fingering.
6. Notice that the same fingers are used in both hands when playing the G major scale in contrary motion.

G MAJOR SCALE—CONTRARY MOTION

Play F♯s as designated by the key signature.

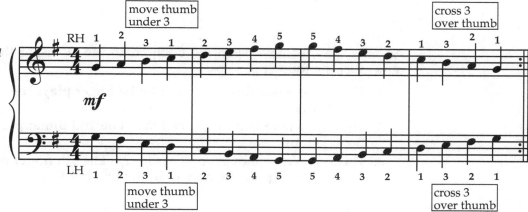

PLAYING THE G MAJOR SCALE IN PARALLEL MOTION

1. Play with hands separately, then with hands together.
2. Use the same suggestions for playing the G major in parallel motion as given for playing the C major scale in contrary motion.
3. Memorize the fingering.
4. The places where both hands use the same finger numbers are bracketed to help you learn the correct fingerings more quickly.

G MAJOR SCALE—PARALLEL MOTION

Play F♯s as designated by the key signature.

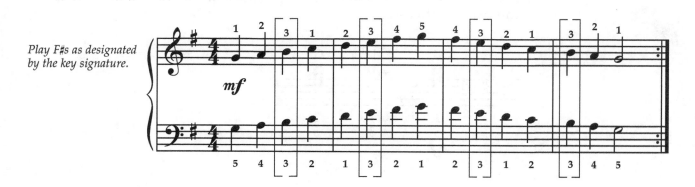

USING THE G MAJOR AND D⁷ CHORDS

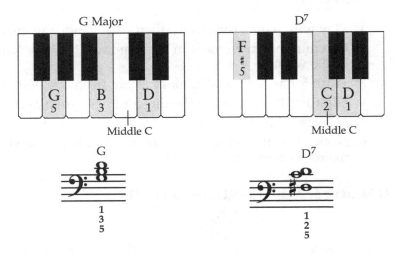

An easy way to move from the G chord to the D⁷ using the left hand is to remember the following steps:

1. The *top* note remains the *same.* **The 1st finger plays the note D in both of the chords.**

2. The *middle* note moves *up a half step.* **The 2nd finger plays the note C in the D⁷ chord.**

3. The *bottom* note moves *down a half step.* **The 5th finger moves out of the G position to play the note F♯ in the D⁷ chord.**

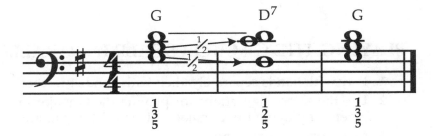

𝒫ractice 𝒮trategies

1. Practice playing the G and D⁷ chord progression with the left hand until you can play it with ease.

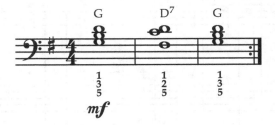

2. Practice the G and D⁷ chord progression with the right hand. **Be sure to use the correct right hand fingering as given.**

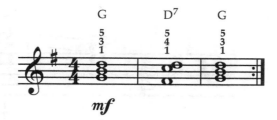

3. Practice the G and D⁷ chord progression with both hands together.

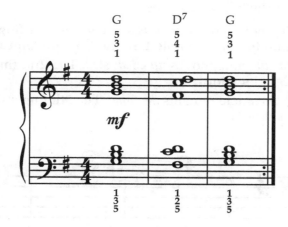

USING THE C MAJOR CHORD IN A NEW POSITION

Instead of playing the C major chord in root position (**C E G**), where C is the lowest note of the C chord, it is easier in the key of G when the C chord is used with **G** as the lowest tone (**G C E**). It still remains a C chord except the order of the three tones has been changed.

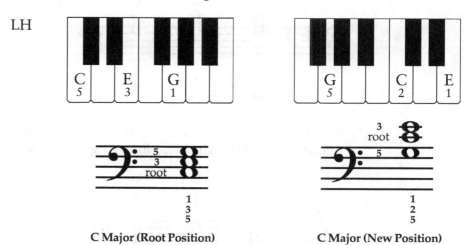

C Major (Root Position)   C Major (New Position)

Notice how much easier it is to move from the G major chord to the C major chord when used in its **G C E** order.

Chord Symbols:

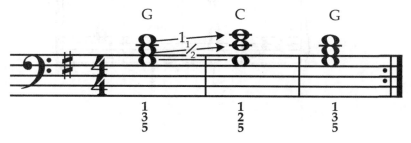

An easy way to move from the G chord to the C chord using the left hand is to remember the following steps:

1. The *top* note moves *up a whole step*. **The 1st finger moves out of the G position to play the note E in the C major chord.**

2. The *middle* note moves *up a half step*. **The 2nd finger plays the note C in the C major chord.**

3. The *bottom* note remains *the same*. **The 5th finger plays the note G in both of the chords.**

![G to C to G chords on bass clef with fingerings 1-3-5, 1-2-5, 1-3-5]

Practice Strategies

1. Practice playing the G and C major chord progression with the left hand until you can play it with ease.

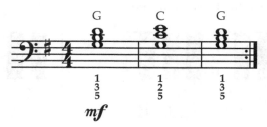

2. Practice the G and C major chord progression with the right hand. **Be sure to use the correct right hand fingerings as given.**

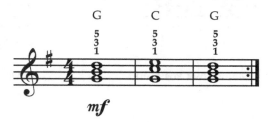

3. Practice the G and C major chord progression with both hands together.

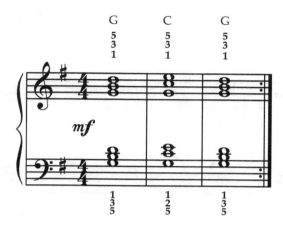

PLAYING THE G MAJOR, C MAJOR, AND D⁷ CHORD PROGRESSION

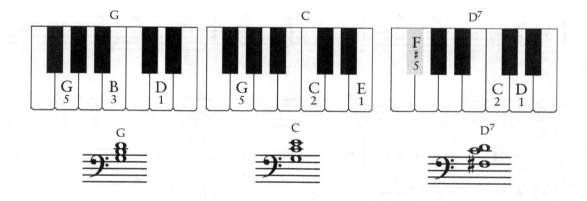

Practice Strategies

Practice playing the G, C, and D⁷ chord progression with each hand separately, and then with both hands together. **Be sure to use the correct fingering as given for both hands.**

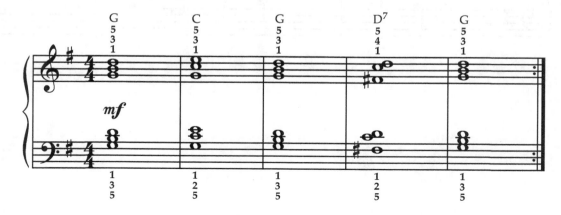

JACOB'S LADDER

Spiritual

ANGELS WE HAVE HEARD ON HIGH

Traditional

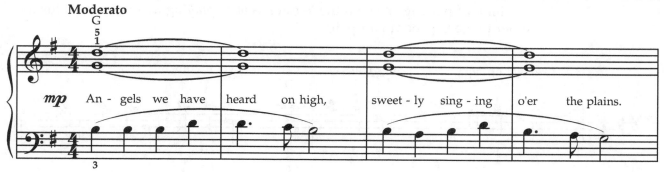

An - gels we have heard on high, sweet - ly sing - ing o'er the plains.

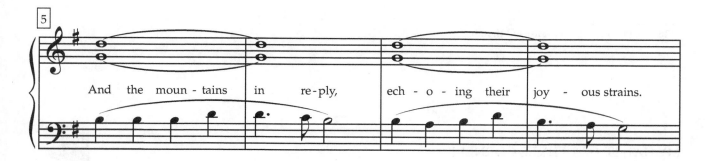

And the moun - tains in re-ply, ech - o - ing their joy - ous strains.

Glo - - - - - - - - - - ri - a,

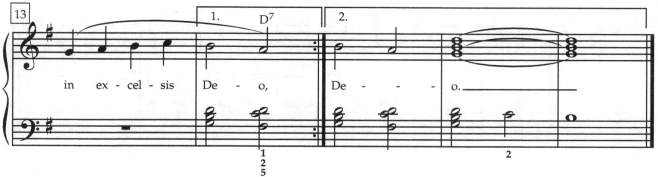

in ex - cel - sis De - o, De - - - o.

PLAYING A WALTZ ACCOMPANIMENT PATTERN

A **waltz pattern** is a broken-chord accompaniment in which the first beat is stressed and the second and third beats are played lightly.

Think of playing *down* on the key for beat 1, playing *up* on the keys for the other two beats (oom-pah-pah).

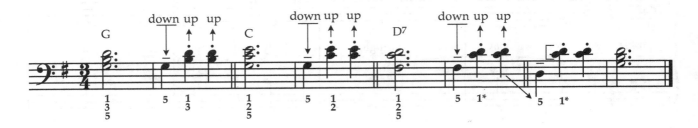

*Take both notes with the left-hand thumb.

MY HAT, IT HAS THREE CORNERS

German

2:21

Tenuto

A marking that means to stress or emphasize a note.

SOLO

RUSSIAN DANCE

*Alexander Goedicke
(1877–1957)*

AMAGING GRACE

Traditional
Arranged by Ken Iversen

2:25

HARMONIZING A LEAD-LINE MELODY

Harmonize the lead-line melody with a block-chord accompaniment using the chords indicated by the letter-name symbols.

DU, DU LIEGST MIR IM HERZEN

German

2:26
MIDI

Harmonize the melody using a waltz accompaniment pattern as illustrated in the first few measures.

DU, DU LIEGST MIR IM HERZEN

German

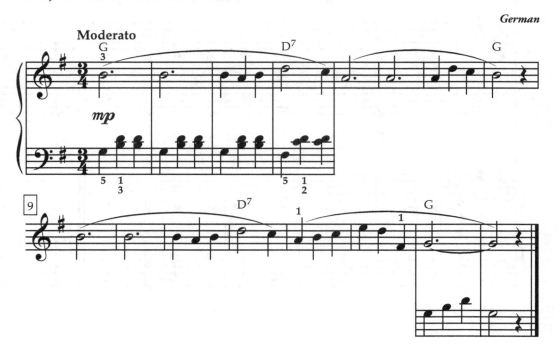

RHYTHMS TO READ

Tap the various rhythmic patterns that follow. The RH taps the notes with the stems going up. The LH taps the notes with the stems going down. First tap each hand separately, and then with both hands together.

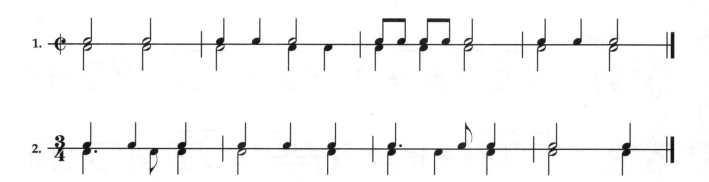

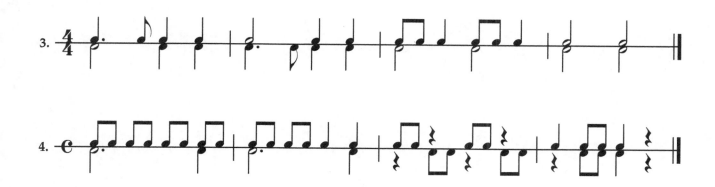

TRAINING THE EAR

Select one of the chord groupings that your teacher plays. The chords played will be G, C, and D^7. Check the correct response on the blanks provided.

NAME _____

DATE _____

SCORE _____

Short Answer

1. Identify the chords that are given. The G, C, and D^7 chords will be used. Place your answers on the blanks provided.

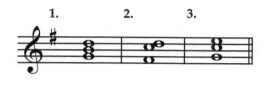

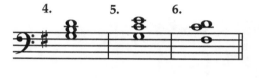

_____   _____   _____   _____   _____   _____

2. Write the correct fingering to the left of each chord.

Construction

3. Write the letter names for the G major scale on the blanks provided.

<u> G </u>   ____   ____   ____   ____   ____   ____   ____

4. Write the key signature for G major on the staves provided.

5. Write the letter names for each of the chords indicated. The first letter name of each chord is given.

G <u> G </u>   ____   ____

C <u> G </u>   ____   ____

D^7 <u> F# </u>   ____   ____

Triads and Chord Inversions

TRIADS OF THE MAJOR SCALE

Triads can be built on every tone of the scale. The sharps and flats must be taken into account in the key signature for that key.

Study the triads built on the two scales that follow, and then play upward, then downward first with the right hand, and then play an octave lower with the left hand.

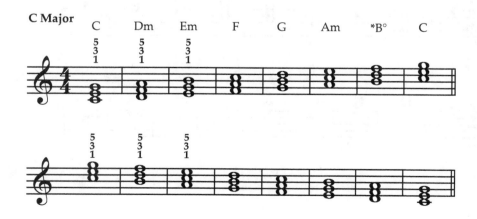

On Another Note...

FRANZ LISZT

Source: Archivo Iconografico, S.A./Corbis

Franz Liszt (1811–1886), renowned Romantic period composer, was born in Hungary where his father was in the service of the Esterhazys, an aristocratic European family that were great patrons of the arts. Liszt was a child prodigy who gained early recognition for his great talent at the piano. His memory was phenomenal—he could hear a piece only once and reproduce all or most of it at the keyboard. Liszt became recognized as one of the greatest of all nineteenth-century concert pianists, and to this day is regarded as perhaps one of the greatest of all time. He was especially known for his ability to play works of immense difficulty because of his tremendous technical skills and power. Consequently, he composed some of the most difficult and demanding piano music ever written. People clamored to hear Liszt play the piano. In fact, it was actually Liszt who started what we know today as the "superstar" system—and that was around 1837! He could not walk down the street without people gathering about him. Ladies wept, screamed, and fainted from excitement and threw bouquets of flowers onto the stage. Adding to the "Lisztomania" was the Liszt ritual of walking out on the stage wearing white gloves. He would then remove his gloves, casting them down at his feet so that his adoring fans could scramble up to the stage to retrieve them. After the frenzy subsided, Liszt would begin his concert. It was Liszt who invented the solo piano recital. He was also a conductor, editor, critic and writer, as well as a master teacher who taught for over forty years—without accepting any payment whatsoever. *"Genie oblige,"* was his motto, which means "we are obliged to give of our talents."

(When playing these triads, remember to play the F♯ as indicated in the key signature given for G major.)

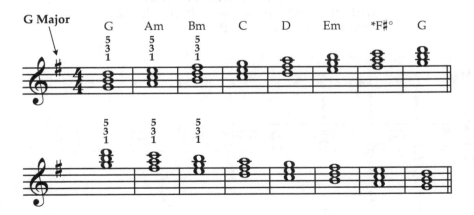

B° is a **diminished** triad. A diminished triad has both the third and fifth tones lowered a half step from its major.

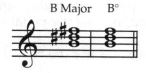

PLAYING ARPEGGIATED CHORDS WITH ALTERNATING HANDS

Play the following major chords as arpeggios (discussed earlier on page 144), alternating from one hand to the other. Then play the study by changing the chords to minor. Remember to lower the middle tone a half step.

Continue to play upward using white keys to begin building the triad (for example: D, E, F, G, and A).

C Major

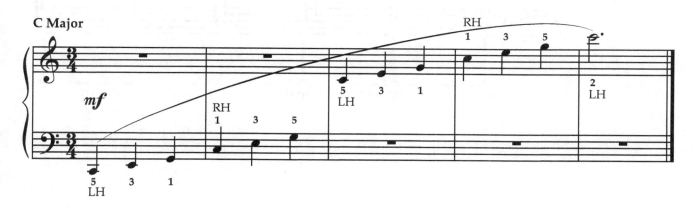

C Minor

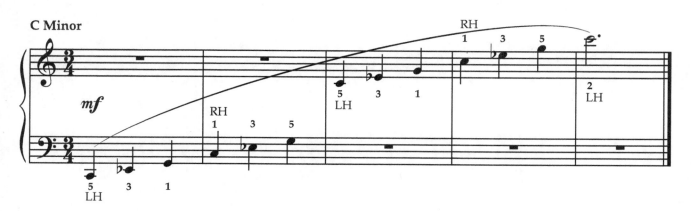

THE DAMPER PEDAL—LEGATO PEDALING

Legato pedaling is used to obtain a very smooth connection of tones. This is created by depressing the damper pedal *immediately after* sounding the chord. As you play each subsequent chord, release the pedal and then press it down again immediately.

Always keep the heel on the floor and use the right foot in an up and down motion.

Legato Pedal Studies

1. Using legato pedaling, practice playing triads on the white keys only.

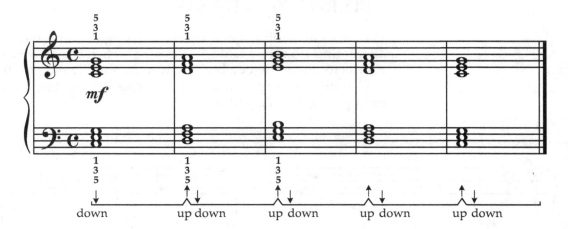

2. Practice the following arpeggiated chords using legato pedaling as indicated.

3. Practice the following chord progression in the key of C major using legato pedaling as indicated.

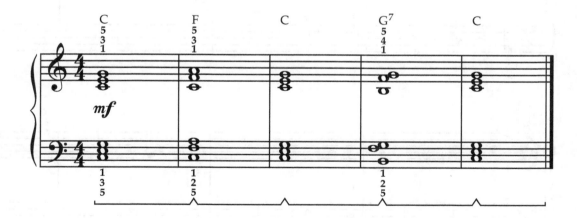

SOLO

SOARING

2:28

Elyse Mach

SOLO

THEN AND NOW

Elyse Mach

CHORD INVERSIONS—TRIADS AND SEVENTH CHORDS

A triad (as discussed earlier on p. 87) consists of three tones—the root, the third, and the fifth. When the root of the triad is located at the bottom of the triad it is in **root position**. A root position triad will have all of its tones arranged in intervals of a third.

A triad is **inverted** when a chord tone other than the root is at the bottom of the chord. An inverted triad will have an interval of a third and an interval of a fourth. When a triad is inverted, the root is the **top note** of the **interval of a fourth**.

Triads may be inverted twice.

When the third of the triad is on the *bottom*, the triad is in **1st inversion**.

When the fifth of the triad is on the *bottom*, the triad is in **2nd inversion**.

The root is shaded in each of the triads shown.

C Major Triad

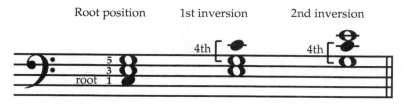

F Major Triad

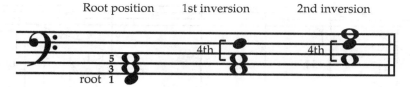

A **seventh chord** consists of four tones—the root, the third, the fifth, and the seventh. For example: the G^7 has four tones: **G B D F.** Seventh chords have three inversions. When the seventh chord is inverted, the root is the **top note** of the **interval of a second**. The root is shaded in each of the seventh chords shown.

G^7 Chord

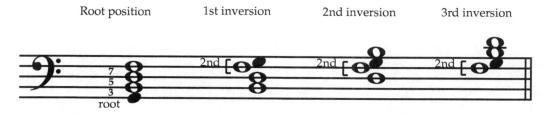

The first inversion* of the G^7 has been the one used throughout this book. Note that the tone D has been omitted to permit more ease in playing this chord at the introductory level.

PLAYING TRIAD INVERSIONS—BLOCKED AND ARPEGGIATED

Practice playing major triads in root position and their inverted positions as given using correct fingerings. First play them blocked and then arpeggiated as illustrated. Then play the triads in minor.

C Major
Root position

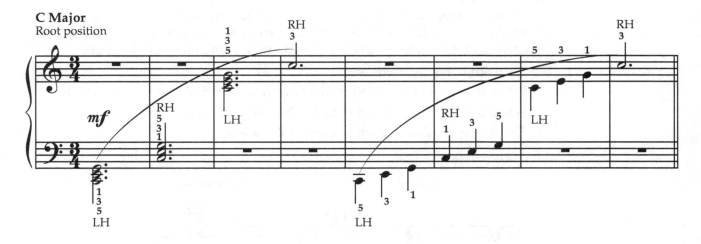

C Major
First inversion

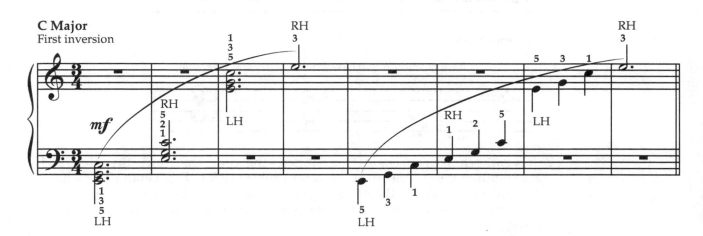

C Major
Second inversion

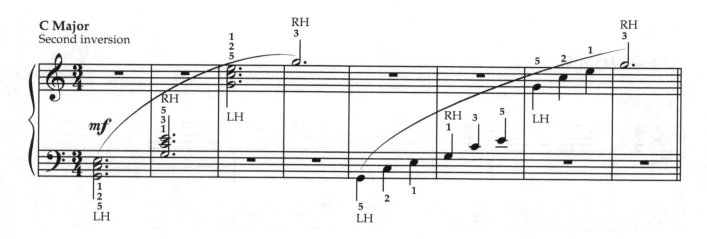

C Minor
Root position

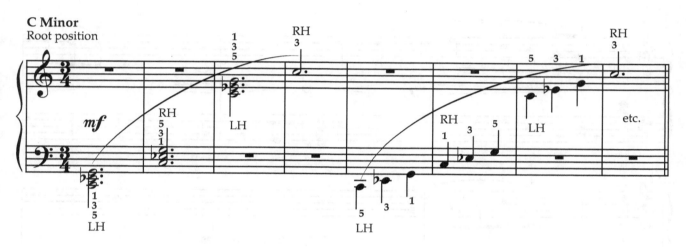

SOLO

CLASSIC DANCE

Phillip Keveren

Allegretto

RHYTHMS TO READ

Tap the various rhythmic patterns that follow. The RH taps the notes with the stems going up. The LH taps the notes with the stems going down. First tap each hand separately, and then with both hands together.

TRAINING THE EAR

Select the correct melodic example that will be played by your teacher. Check the correct response on the blanks provided.

NAME ————————————
DATE ————————————
SCORE ————————————

Short Answer

1. Identify the triads given by their letter name symbols (i.e., G for G major and Gm for G minor). Place your answers on the blanks provided.

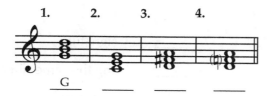

G —— —— —— ——   —— —— —— ——

2. Identify the chords by letter name in their inverted position. Then indicate whether the chord is in 1st inversion (use 1st) or 2nd inversion (use 2nd). Place your answers on the blanks provided.

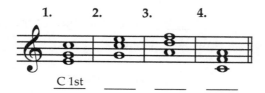

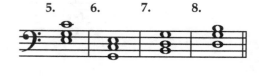

C 1st —— —— ——   —— —— —— ——

Construction

3. Build the triads indicated by the letter-name symbols given.

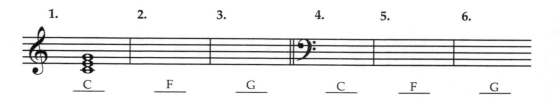

C   F   G   C   F   G

Matching

Write the numbers from Column A to correspond to the given answers in Column B.

COLUMN A	COLUMN B
1. primary chords	_____ moving the opposite direction
2. parallel motion	_____ 1½ beats
3. AB form	_____ key signature
4. ABA form	_____ moving the same direction
5. ⌊_____⋀_____⌋	_____ legato pedaling
6. contrary motion	_____ 3 beats
7. root position	_____ when the fifth of the chord is in the bass
8. (treble clef with one sharp)	_____ when the third of the chord is in the bass
9. first inversion	_____ two-part form
10. second inversion	_____ three-part form
11. ♩.	_____ C, F, and G chords in C major
12. 𝅗𝅥.	_____ the root is at the bottom of the chord

Reading in F Major

THE F MAJOR SCALE

The **F major scale** has eight tones with half steps between A–B♭ and E–F, and with whole steps between all of the other tones. The B♭ (flat) is used to preserve the pattern of whole steps and half steps of the F major scale.

When a piece is based on the F major scale, it is written in the **key** of F major.

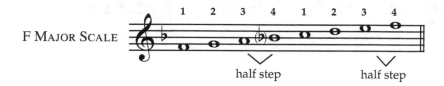

F MAJOR SCALE

The **key signature** is the B♭ located at the beginning of each staff. It indicates that every B in the key of F major will be played as B♭ throughout the piece.

THE F MAJOR SCALE IN TETRACHORD POSITION

The left hand will start on F to build the first four-note tetrachord pattern and the right hand will start on C to build the second four note tetrachord. Remember that a whole step joins the two tetrachords.

F Major Scale in Tetrachord Position

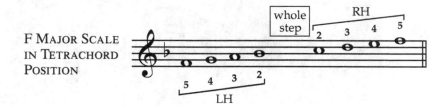

Practice Strategies

Practice playing the following warm-up scale preparation exercises.

1.

2.

3.

4.

PLAYING THE F MAJOR SCALE IN PARALLEL MOTION

1. Play with hands separately, then with hands together.
2. Use minimal movement in the hands and wrists. No twisting or turning of the wrists.
3. Work for an even and smooth legato moving from one note to the next.
4. Slightly tilt the hand in the direction you are playing.
5. Memorize the fingering.
6. The places where both hands use the same finger numbers are bracketed to help you learn the correct fingerings more quickly.

Play B♭s as designated by the key signature.

F MAJOR SCALE— PARALLEL MOTION

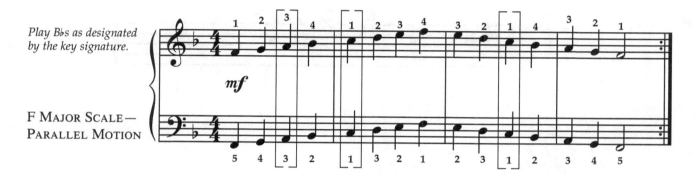

USING THE F MAJOR, B♭ MAJOR, AND C⁷ CHORDS

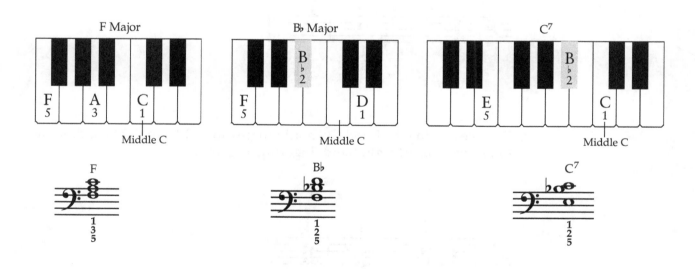

An easy way to move from the F chord to the C⁷ chord using the left hand is to remember the following steps:

1. The *top* note remains the *same*. **The 1st finger plays the note C in both of the chords.**

2. The *middle* note moves *up a half step*. **The 2nd finger plays the note B♭ in the C⁷ chord.**

3. The *bottom* note moves *down a half step*. **The 5th finger moves out of the F position to play the note E in the C⁷ chord.**

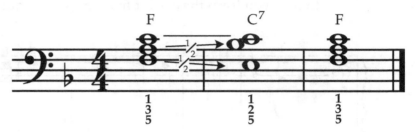

Practice Strategies

1. Practice playing the F and C⁷ chord progression with the left hand until you can play it with ease.

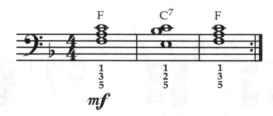

2. Practice playing the F and C⁷ chord progression with the right hand. **Be sure to use the correct right hand fingering as given.**

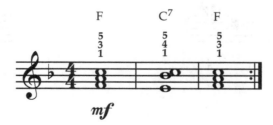

3. Practice playing the F and C^7 chord progression with both hands together.

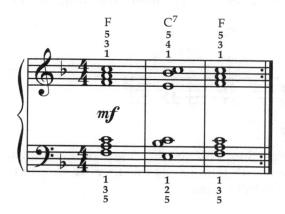

An easy way to move from the F chord to the B♭ chord using the left hand is to remember these following steps:

1. The *top* note moves *up a whole step*. **The 1st finger moves out of the F position to play the note D in the B♭ major chord.**

2. The *middle* note moves *up a half step*. **The 2nd finger plays the B♭ in the B♭ major chord.**

3. The *bottom* note remains *the same*. **The 5th finger plays the note F in both of the chords.**

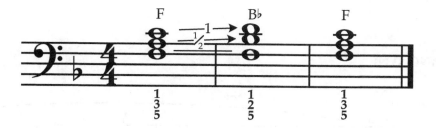

Practice Strategies

1. Practice playing the F and B♭ major chord progression with the left hand until you can play it with ease.

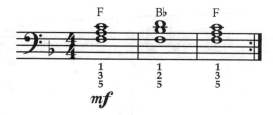

2. Practice playing the F and B♭ major chord progression with the right hand. **Be sure to use the correct right hand fingerings as given.**

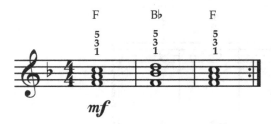

3. Practice playing the F, B♭, and C⁷ chord progression with each hand separately, and then with both hands together. **Be sure to use the correct fingering as given for both hands.**

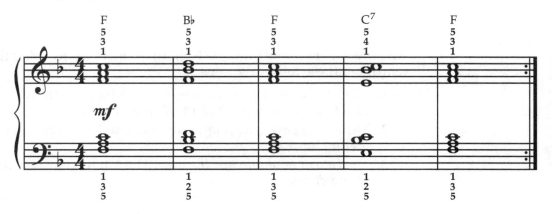

AULD LANG SYNE

Scottish

Franz Liszt *Romantic period composer/pianist/teacher*

Create Memories.

PLAYING THE ALBERTI BASS ACCOMPANIMENT PATTERN

Alberti Bass

The Alberti bass is an accompaniment pattern using a repeated arpeggio arranged in the following order:

- lowest tone
- highest tone
- middle tone
- highest tone

It is named after the Baroque composer Domenico Alberti, who used this kind of accompaniment in his music, as did later Classical composers.

SEMPRE STACCATO

The term **sempre staccato** means "always staccato." Note that staccato dots are unnecessary with this instruction.

AH, VOUS DIRAI-JE, MAMAN? *(Ah, Shall I Tell You, Mama?)*

French

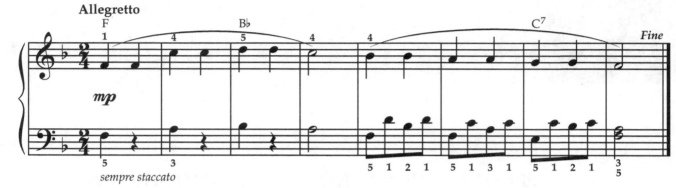

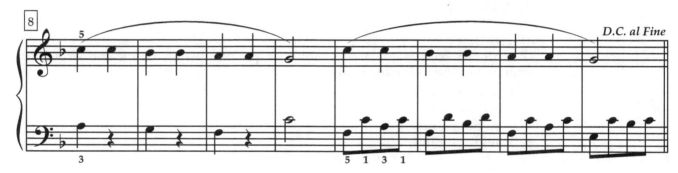

HARMONIZING A LEAD-LINE MELODY

Harmonize the lead-line melody with a block-chord accompaniment using the chords indicated by the letter-name symbols.

2:38

NEW RIVER TRAIN

American

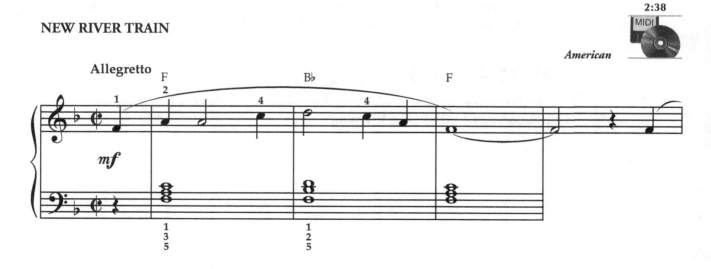

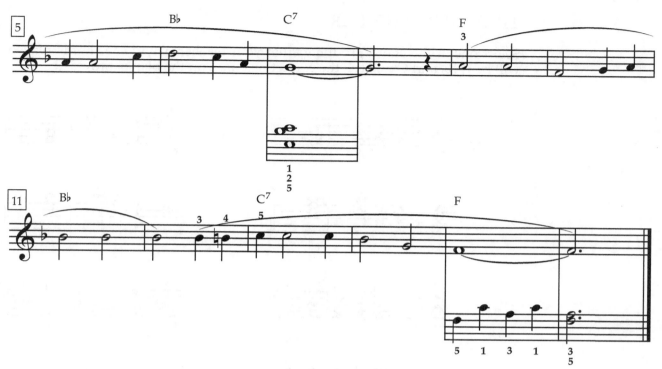

Harmonize the melody using an Alberti bass accompaniment pattern as illustrated in the first few measures.

NEW RIVER TRAIN

American

TRAINING THE EAR

Select one of the chord groupings that your teacher plays. The chords played
will be F, B♭, and C^7. Check the correct response on the blanks provided.

NAME _____

DATE _____

SCORE _____

Short Answer

1. Identify the chords that are given. The F, B♭, and C⁷ chords will be used. Place your answers on the blanks provided.

___ ___ ___   ___ ___ ___

2. Write the correct fingering to the left of each chord.

Construction

3. Write the letter names for the F major scale.

 F   ___   ___   ___   ___   ___   ___   ___

4. Write the key signature for F major on the staves provided.

5. Write the letter names for each of the chords indicated. The first letter name of each chord is given.

F   F   ___   ___

B♭   F   ___   ___

C⁷   E   ___   ___

Definition

6. Define the following terms:

   a. tenuto _____

   _____

   b. sempre staccato _____

   _____

   c. Alberti bass _____

   _____

The Minor Scale

THE RELATIVE MINOR SCALE

For each major key, there is a corresponding minor key called the **relative minor.** Both keys use the same key signature. The minor scale uses as its starting note the sixth tone of the major scale. Another way the minor scale can be formed is by beginning *three half steps down from the relative major key.*

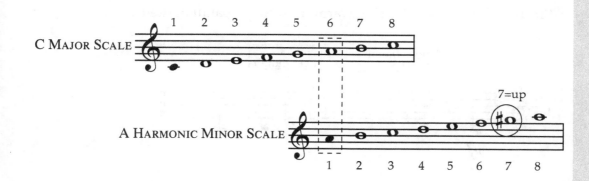

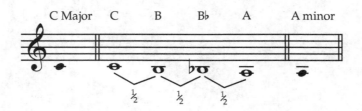

THE HARMONIC MINOR SCALE

There are three forms of the minor scale but the one that is most frequently used is the **harmonic minor.** The harmonic minor scale uses the same tones as the major scale (referred to as its **relative major**), except that the seventh tone of the harmonic minor scale is raised one half step (remember it as 7-up) with the use of an accidental, as shown in the previous scale.

THE A HARMONIC MINOR SCALE IN TETRACHORD POSITION

An easy way to start playing the A harmonic minor scale is by using four fingers (no thumbs) in each hand to build the two tetrachords.

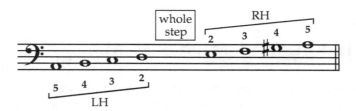

𝒫ractice 𝒮trategies

Practice playing the following warm-up scale preparation exercises.

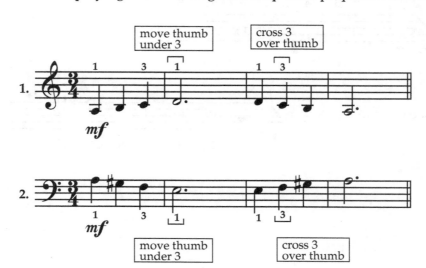

PLAYING THE A HARMONIC MINOR SCALE IN CONTRARY MOTION

1. Play with hands separately, then with both hands together.
2. Use minimal movement in the hands and wrists. No twisting or turning of the wrists.
3. Work for an even and smooth legato from one note to the next.
4. Slightly tilt the hand in the direction you are playing.
5. Memorize the fingering.
6. Notice that the same fingers are used in both hands when playing the A harmonic minor scale in contrary motion.

A HARMONIC MINOR SCALE—CONTRARY MOTION

PLAYING THE A HARMONIC MINOR SCALE IN PARALLEL MOTION

1. Play with hands separately, then with both hands together.
2. Use the same suggestions for playing the A harmonic minor scale in parallel motion as given for playing the A harmonic minor scale in contrary motion.
3. Memorize the fingering.
4. The places where both hands use the same finger numbers are bracketed to help you learn the correct fingerings more quickly.

A HARMONIC MINOR SCALE—PARALLEL MOTION

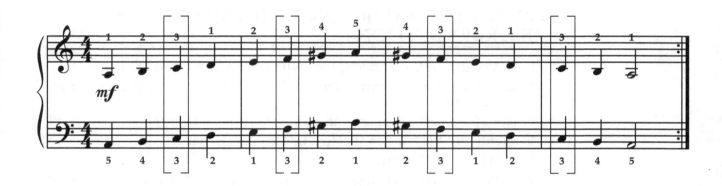

PLAYING THE i, iv, AND V^7 CHORDS IN A MINOR

Since the i and iv chords are minor, small Roman numerals are used to indicate that they are minor.

Practice Strategies

Practice the Am, Dm, and E^7 chord progression with hands separately, and then with both hands together.

SOLO

MOROCCAN SANDS

2:40

Elyse Mach

PRELUDE

In the nineteenth century, a **prelude** was a short instrumental piece, independent in style using a free form. It was usually written for the piano.

Molto

Molto means very, or much.

SOLO

PRELUDE

2:42

Elyse Mach

SCARBOROUGH FAIR

English

2:44
MIDI

Moderato

mf

mp

rit.

SOLO

CAROL OF THE BELLS

Mykola Leontovych
(1877–1921)

PRELUDE (*from* The Children's Musical Friend)

Heinrich Wohlfahrt (1797–1883)
Op. 87, No. 2

Lento

(RH one octave higher than written throughout)

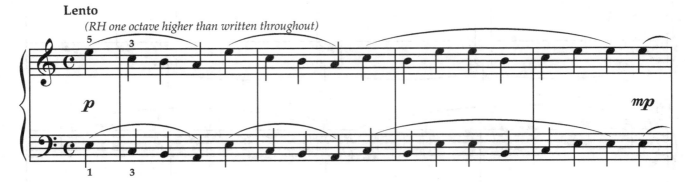

(LH two octaves higher than written throughout)

PRELUDE (*from* The Children's Musical Friend)

Accompaniment

Heinrich Wohlfahrt (1797–1883)
Op. 87, No. 2

Lento

HARMONIZING A LEAD-LINE MELODY

Harmonize the lead-line melody with a block-chord accompaniment using the chords indicated by the letter-name symbols.

UKRAINIAN FOLK SONG

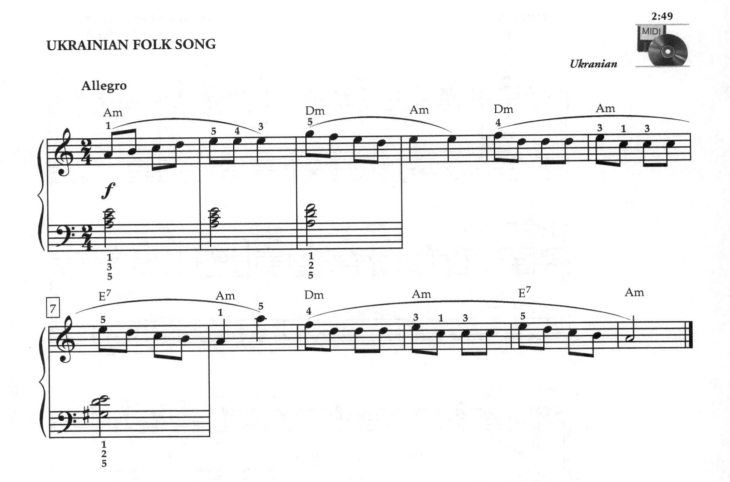

Harmonize the melody using a broken-chord accompaniment pattern as illustrated in the first few measures.

UKRAINIAN FOLK SONG

Ukrainian

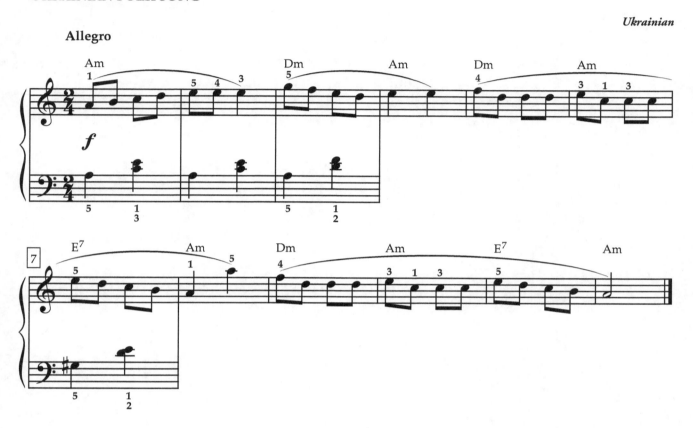

NAME _____

DATE _____

SCORE _____

Short Answer

1. Identify the chords that are given. The Am, Dm, and E^7 chords will be used. Place your answers on the blanks provided.

_____   _____   _____   _____   _____

2. Write the correct fingering to the left of each chord.

Construction

3. Write the letter names for each of the four scales given to the left of each note. Above the notes for each scale write in the RH fingering, and below each scale write the LH fingering.

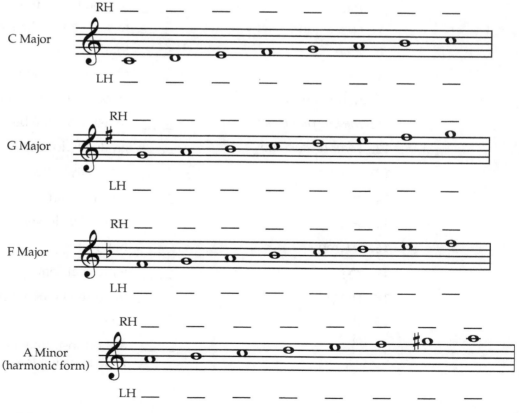

4. Write the letter names for each of the chords indicated. The first letter name of each chord is given.

Am   <u> A </u>   <u>   </u>   <u>   </u>

Dm   <u> A </u>   <u>   </u>   <u>   </u>

E^7   <u> G♯ </u>   <u>   </u>   <u>   </u>

Matching

Write the numbers from Column A to correspond to the given answers in Column B.

COLUMN A	COLUMN B
1. interval	_____ lowers a tone a half step
2. legato	_____ return to the original tempo
3. ritardando	_____ very, or much
4. phrase	_____ always staccato
5. prelude	_____ to hold longer than the given value
6. *forte* (*f*)	_____ moderately soft
7. crescendo	_____ raises a tone a half step higher
8. *Fine*	_____ loud
9. molto	_____ short or detached
10. diminuendo	_____ smooth and connected
11. *mezzo piano* (*mp*)	_____ repeat from the beginning
12. *sempre staccato*	_____ gradually louder
13. staccato	_____ gradually softer
14. ▬	_____ finish or end
15. ▬	_____ gradually slower
16. a tempo	_____ half rest
17. ⌒	_____ a musical sentence
18. sharp (♯)	_____ the distance between two tones
19. flat (♭)	_____ whole rest
20. :‖	_____ a short instrumental piece independent in style, using free form

Exploring the Twentieth Century

BLUES

The musical style known as the Blues was born around the turn of the twentieth century. Blues is known for its lamenting, melancholy melody. The 12-bar blues is based on a twelve measure harmonic pattern. Using block chords in the left hand, play the harmonic pattern as given holding each chord for four beats:

$\frac{4}{4}$

C	C	C	C
F	F	C	C
G	F	C	C

On Another Note...

THE ELECTRONIC KEYBOARD

In the late twentieth century, technology brought about the electronic keyboard. Unlike the piano, it has neither hammers nor strings. Instead, the key activates sounds digitally programmed on a microchip. The sound produced can only be heard through an amplifier or earphones.

The **blues scale** is made up of the lowered third, fifth, and seventh tones of a major scale.

THE BLUES SCALE

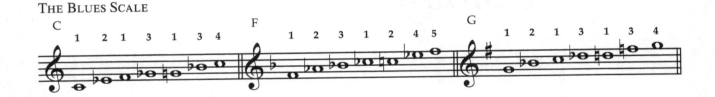

Practice playing the five-finger blues pattern (the first five notes of the blues scale) before putting the five-finger blues pattern with the 12 bar blues chord progression.

FIVE-FINGER BLUES PATTERN

same key
F♯ or G♭

SOLO

WINDY CITY BLUES

Elyse Mach

TRANSCENDENTAL BLUES

Ken Iversen

2:53

*Suggestion: The pair of eighth notes [♫] may be played so that the first eighth note is held a little longer and the second eighth note is held a bit shorter to give it a jazzier effect.

longer | shorter

RAGTIME

Ragtime is characterized by a steady, marchlike accompaniment in the left hand. The right hand plays a decorated, syncopated melody that sounds as if it had "ragged" rhythmic edges—and so this style of piano music was dubbed ragtime.

On Another Note...

SCOTT JOPLIN

Source: Portrait of American ragtime composer and pianist Scott Joplin (1868–1917), circa 1910. Photo by Frank Driggs Collection/Getty Images.

Scott Joplin (1868–1917) was born near Linden, Texas, the son of an ex-slave. At the early age of 7, Joplin already showed an extraordinary talent for music. He learned how to play the piano by visiting and then later playing in "honky-tonk" establishments. Along the way he developed his own compositional style. He began writing down some of the pieces he performed, and over a period of time some were published. One of the first compositions he published was *Original Rags* in 1899. Soon afterward he followed it with his best known composition, *Maple Leaf Rag.* Over time Joplin became known as the "King of Ragtime." This style of music is highly syncopated. Its features are a steady bass line with a highly syncopated melody above it. Joplin's melodies were so syncopated that this type of music originally dubbed "ragged time," later grew to be "ragtime" or "rag" music. *The Entertainer* is an example of rag music. Joplin did not receive recognition as a serious composer until 50 years after his death. Then in 1974, with the movie *The Sting,* which featured arrangements of many of Joplin's rags, *The Entertainer* became an overnight success that could be heard and played everywhere. In 1976, three years later, Joplin's opera *Treemonisha* was awarded the coveted Pulitzer Prize.

WHAT TIME? RAGTIME

Ken Iversen

JAZZ

New Orleans was the major center of jazz around the beginning of the twentieth century. **Jazz** has been one of the most influential musical styles in the twentieth century. Some of the basic style elements of jazz include: syncopation, off-beat accents, and chromaticism.

JUST STRUTTIN' ALONG

Martha Mier

TWENTIETH-CENTURY CLASSICS

THE BEAR

Vladimir Rebikoff
(1866–1920)

On Another Note...

THE CONTEMPORARY PERIOD (1900 TO PRESENT)

Source: Picasso, Pablo (1881–1973) © ARS, NY. Three Musicians, 1921. The Philadelphia Museum of Art/Art Resource, NY.

The need in music to try something fresh and different led to many new musical styles during the time frame of 1900 to the present. Since composers seemed to have had such a need to develop their own unique styles, their styles could often change with each of the new compositions they wrote. Jazz, ragtime, atonal music, electronic music, minimalism, and aleatoric (chance) music are just a few of the multitude of musical styles of this "Anything Goes" period.

Dissonance, unique sound production and sound "fusions," twentieth-century notations and expressions are prevalent. The piano is sometimes used more as a percussive instrument rather than a string instrument. Prepared piano, the toy piano, as well as the interior and exterior elements of the piano are utilized in the music-making process. Electronic keyboards, digital pianos and synthesizers are used as well. Traditional styles of composition for the piano, that were also used in prior historical periods, include sonatas, preludes and fugues, dance suites, character pieces, toccatas, theme and variations, and a variety of free forms. Scott Joplin, George Gershwin, Igor Stravinsky, Aaron Copland, Dmitri Kabalevsky, Béla Bartók, Samuel Barber, and John Cage are prominent composers of this period.

SPRINGTIME SONG (*No. 2 from* For Children, *Vol. 1*)

Béla Bartók
(1881–1945)

SCHERZANDO

Scherzando is a tempo marking that means to play in a joking manner.

A LITTLE JOKE

2:63

Dmitri Kabalevsky
(1904–1987)

INNOVATIVE NOTATIONS

An **innovative notation** is any notation invented by a composer to indicate special effects and how they should be performed. In *Seashore,* the white stemmed rectangles are dotted half note clusters. The number [5] that appears above the rectangles specifies the number of tones, and the positions of the rectangles on the staff specify the exact pitches.

PRACTICE DIRECTIONS

Six components make up the piece *Seashore.*
1. Study and play each of these components.
2. Tap out the rhythms of the piece.
3. Play the piece as written

15*ma*

The marking **15*ma*** indicates to play 15 notes (two octaves) higher than written.

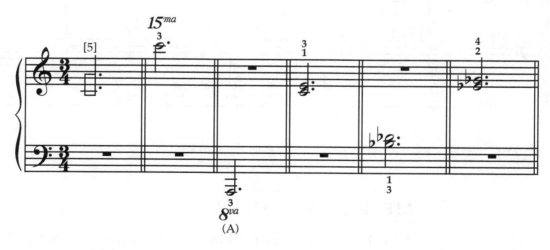

SEASHORE

Ross Lee Finney
(1906–1997)

METRONOME MARK

♩ = **120** is a **metronome marking.** A metronome is a time-keeping device which produces a ticking sound at any desired speed. This particular marking means to set the metronome at 120, with the resulting ticking sound equal to the time it should take to play each quarter note.

QUARTAL HARMONY

Quartal harmony is based on chords built in fourths rather than in the traditional thirds. In *The Cathedral in the Snow,* which uses an old Christmas chant, the whole-note figures are in quartal harmony. Other contemporary features are the omission of a time signature and bar lines, and the use of tones that are blurred together for effect by holding the pedal down for the duration of the piece.

THE CATHEDRAL IN THE SNOW *(A Gregorian Christmas Chant)*

David Duke

Very slowly

Continued

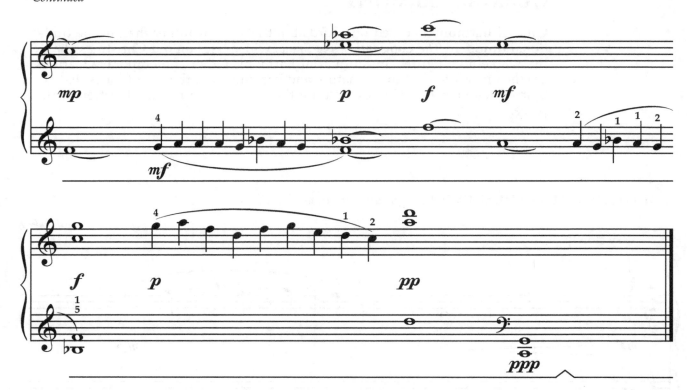

BLACK AND WHITE

Piano 1: White-key cluster—use C–D–E played together.
Piano 2: Black-key cluster—use G♭ –A♭ –B♭ played together.

André Watts *concert pianist*

On technique: What helps is to dissect a really difficult passage—one that has a lot of notes—away from the keyboard. Don't dissect it by playing it again and again or by playing it slower. Get away from the piano, and if you know what the notes are, don't even look at the score. Envision the notes as you would envision a dancer taking steps. Find out how you're playing—what note it is—what you always miss or which note it is that doesn't always speak or that speaks too much. Then find a motion to correct it. For instance, know that you must give a little extra to the right side of the hand with the fourth finger when you get to that place, or whatever.

Source: Photo by Christian Steiner. Courtesy of Indiana University.

IMPROVISATION

12-Bar Blues

Practice the left hand pattern as given next that uses the major chords of C, F, and G. Then begin improvising a pattern in the right hand that melodically uses the tones of the major chords of C, F, and G, **and** includes the **blue note**—a lowered third (minor third).

The first few measures of the improvisation are written out to help you get started.

MOVIN' ON BLUES

Elyse Mach

Numerous blues melodies can be improvised by changing the note combinations and using a variety of rhythm patterns. Here are just a few ways of playing the same melody with several different rhythm patterns that you can use in improvising your own 12-bar blues.

12-BAR BLUES MELODY EXAMPLES

More Repertoire to Play

On Another Note...

FACING THE MUSIC

As a young pianist Vladimir Horowitz was once given a word of advice by noted concert pianist, Artur Schnabel. Said Schnabel: "When a piece gets difficult, make faces."

FOUR MINIATURE CLASSICS

MARCH

2:68

Daniel Gottlob Türk
(1750–1813)

MELODY

2:70

Louis Köhler
(1820–1886)

DANCE

Dmitri Kabalevsky
(1904–1987)

MOVING AROUND

Dmitri Kabalevsky

VIVACE

Cornelius Gurlitt, Op. 117, No. 8
(1829–1901)

FÜR ELISE

Ludwig van Beethoven (1770–1827)
Arranged by Elyse Mach

Continued

An **écossaise** is a dance lively in character that uses two beats to the measure.

ÉCOSSAISE

2:80

Franz Schubert
(1797–1828)

THE ENTERTAINER

Scott Joplin (1868–1917)
Arranged by Elyse Mach

A FIRST NOCTURNE (*for Tiffany Oliver*)

Rick Robertson

RAZZ-MA-TAZZ

WONDERING

Phillip Keveren

Reflectively

Continued

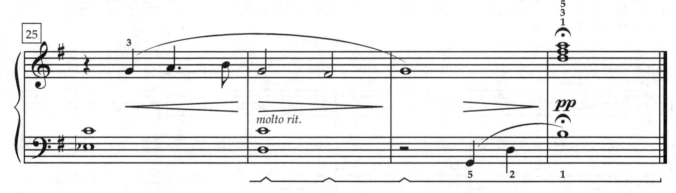

Glossary Terms

Accent sign (>) a sign placed over or under a note to indicate stress or emphasis

Adagio rather slow

Alla breve (¢) cut time or 2/2 time

Allegretto moderately fast

Andante at a walking pace

Arpeggio a broken chord; pitches are sounded one after another rather than simultaneously

A tempo return to the original tempo

Binary form (AB) a piece that is divided into two sections: A and B

Chromatic scale a scale entirely made up of half steps

Clef indicates the pitches of the notes

  Treble clef (𝄞) also called the G clef because it circles around the second line of the staff and designates that line as the note G

  Bass clef (𝄢) also called the F clef because the fourth staff line is enclosed by dots, designating that line as the note F

Coda a concluding section of a few measures at the end of the piece

Coda sign (⊕) indicates to move to the coda

Common time (C) the same as 4/4 time

Crescendo (<) gradually becoming louder

Cut time (¢) the same as 2/2 time; alla breve

Da capo al coda (D.C. al coda) repeat from the beginning to ⊕, then skip to the coda

Da capo al fine (D.C. al fine) repeat from the beginning to *Fine,* the finish or end

Dal segno al fine (D.S. al fine) repeat from the sign ℅ to *Fine*

Damper pedal the right pedal

Decrescendo (>) gradually becoming softer

Diminuendo (>) gradually becoming softer

Dominant the fifth tone of a major or minor scale

Downbeat starting on the first beat of the measure

Dynamics the softness or loudness of a tone

Fermata (⌢) indicates a hold or pause; hold the note under the sign a longer time than its full value

Fine the end

First ending ⌐1. play the first time only

Flat sign (♭) a sign indicating to play the note one key to the left

Forte (f) loud

Fortissimo (ff) very loud

Grand staff the joining of the treble and bass clefs

Half step from one key to the very next key upward or downward

Harmonic interval the distance between two tones that are sounded together

Incomplete measure the beginning measure of a piece has fewer beats than indicated in the time signature. Usually the missing beats are found in the last measure

Interval the distance between two tones

Inversion the rearrangement of the tones of a chord that has the root appearing in one of the upper positions

Key signature the sharps and flats indicating the key of the piece, written at the beginning of each line

Legato smooth and connected

Leger line lines used above or below a staff to extend the range of notes

Major chord the first, third, and fifth tones of the major scale sounded together

Melodic intervals the distance between two tones that are played separately

Mezzo forte (***mf***)   moderately loud

Mezzo piano (***mp***)   moderately soft

Moderato   at a moderate tempo

Molto   much

Moto   motion

Natural sign (♮)   a sign that cancels a sharp or flat and indicates that the note is to be played in its natural state

Octave   every key with the same letter name eight tones higher or lower

Octave higher *8va* ⁓⁓⁓⁓⁓   play one octave higher than written

Octave lower *8va* ....   play one octave lower than written

Pedal marking (└────┘)   press down the damper pedal, hold, and then release it

Phrase   a musical thought or sentence

Pianissimo (***pp***)   very soft

Piano (***p***)   soft

Poco   a little

Poco moto   a little motion

Repeat sign (:‖)   play the piece or section a second time

Rests   signs for silence

Rhythm   the arrangement of note values

Ritardando (**rit.**)   gradually becoming slower

Root   the bottom tone of an interval or triad

Root position   when the root of a chord is used at the bottom of the chord

Second ending |2.‾‾‾‾   play the second time only

Sharp sign (♯)   a sign indicating to play the note one key to the right

Simile   in the same manner

Slur   to play the notes within the curved line *legato*

Staccato ♩ ♩   notes with dots under or above indicating to play short and detached

Subdominant   the fourth tone of a major or minor scale

Subito   suddenly; at once

Tempo   the rate of speed

Ternary form (ABA)   a piece divided into a three-part form: A–B–A

Tetrachord   a series of four tones consisting of two whole steps and a half step

Tie   a curved line which connects notes on the same line or space and is held for the combined values of both notes

Time signature   two numbers at the beginning of a piece that looks like a fraction. The top number indicates the number of beats in a measure. The bottom number indicates the kind of note that receives the beat

Tonic chord   the first, third, and fifth tones are built on the first note of a major or minor scale and sounded together

Transposition   to play the same music in a different key

Triad   a three-tone chord that is built in intervals of a third—a root with a third and a fifth above

Upbeat   a piece that begins with an incomplete measure; it does not begin on the first beat

Vivace   quick; spirited

Whole step   an interval made of two half steps; skip one key in moving from one key to the next

ASSIGNMENT SHEETS

UNIT 1   Keyboard Introduction

_____
_____
_____
_____
_____
_____
_____
_____
_____

UNIT 2   Playing Melodies Using Different Positions

_____
_____
_____
_____
_____
_____
_____
_____
_____

UNIT 3 Reading Music

_____

_____

_____

_____

_____

_____

_____

_____

UNIT 4 More Reading Basics

_____

_____

_____

_____

_____

_____

_____

_____

_____

UNIT 5   Major Five-Finger Patterns and Major Triads

_____

_____

_____

_____

_____

_____

_____

_____

_____

_____

UNIT 6   Minor Five-Finger Patterns and Minor Triads

_____

_____

_____

_____

_____

_____

_____

_____

_____

_____

UNIT 7 Harmonizing Melodies

_____

_____

_____

_____

_____

_____

_____

_____

UNIT 8 The Major Scale/Reading in C Major

_____

_____

_____

_____

_____

_____

_____

_____

_____

_____

UNIT 9 Reading in G Major

_____

_____

_____

_____

_____

_____

_____

_____

UNIT 10 Triads and Chord Inversions

_____

_____

_____

_____

_____

_____

_____

_____

_____

UNIT 11   Reading in F Major

_____

_____

_____

_____

_____

_____

_____

_____

UNIT 12   The Minor Scale

_____

_____

_____

_____

_____

_____

_____

_____

_____

UNIT 13 Exploring the Twentieth Century

UNIT 14 More Repertoire to Play

Title Index

Aaron's Song (Peirick), 106–107
Acaba, 70–71
Ah, Vous Dirai-Je, Maman?, 198
Alleluia, 133
Amazing Grace, 168–169
Angels We Have Heard on High, 165
Au Clair De La Lune, 24–25
Auld Lang Syne, 196

Bear, The (Rebikoff), 228–229
Beautiful Brown Eyes, 152
Bells of London, 114
Black and White, 237
Bouncy, 19

Canon (Pachelbel), 130–132
Carol of the Bells (Leontovych), 210–211
Casey Jones, 92
Cathedral in the Snow, The (Duke), 235–236
Chickalileeo, 103
Chimes Afar, 50
Classic Dance, 186
Classic Twist, 146–147
Country Tune, 52

Dance (Kabalevsky), 243
Dialogue, 66
Distant Shores, 9
Dorian Four, 33–34
Du, Du Liegst Mir Im Herzen, 169–170

Écossaise (Schubert), 247
Entertainer, The (Joplin), 248–249

Fanfare, 76
First Nocturne, A (Robertson), 250–251
French Folk Song, 96–97
Für Elise (Beethoven), 245–246

German Folk Song, 114
Gliding, 48

Jacob's Ladder, 164
Jazz Waltz, A, 30
Jingle Bells (Pierpont), 120–121
Just Struttin' Along (Mier), 226–227

Kum Ba Yah, 122–123

Landmark Pairs, 42–43
Latin Moves, 69
Little Joke, A (Kabalevsky), 232
Love Somebody, 46

March (Türk), 242
Mary Ann, 113
Melody (Diabelli), 56
Melody (Köhler), 242
Michael, Row the Boat Ashore, 144
Monday Blues, 72
Moonlit Sea, 128
Moroccan Sands, 207
Moving Around (Kabalevsky), 243
Movin' on Blues, 238–239
Musette (Bach), 93
My Hat, It Has Three Corners, 166

Navajo Chant, 64–65
New River Train, 198–199

Ode to Joy (Beethoven), 26
Ole!, 73
On Top of Old Smoky, 145

Perpetual Rock, 124–125
Prelude, 208
Prelude (Wohlfahrt), 212–213

Razzle Dazzle (Evans), 77–78
Razz-Ma-Tazz (Olson), 252
Remembering, 15
Reverie, 102
Rock My Soul, 16–17
Russian Dance (Goedicke), 167

Saigon Traffic, 10–11
Sakura, 18
Scale Study No. 1, 142
Scale Study No. 2, 143
Scarborough Fair, 209
Scottish Highlands, 129
Seashore (Finney), 234
Shall We Gather at the River (Lowry), 94
Shepherd's Song (Beethoven), 32
Shoestring Boogie, 74–75
Shortenin' Bread, 68
Sixth Degree, 149
Soaring, 180–181
Song of Praise, 95
Spring (Vivaldi), 107–108
Springtime Song (Bartók), 230–231
Stepping Along, 44–45
Stepping Down in C, 63

Stepping Up in C, 62
Swing, 53

Then and Now, 182
Time-Clock Blues, 126
Transcendental Blues, 222

Ukrainian Folk Song, 214–215
Urubamba Majesty, 151

Vivace (Gurlitt), 244

What Time? Ragtime, 224–225
When the Saints Go Marching In, 54–55
Whistle Daughter, 28
Windy City Blues, 221
Wondering, 253–254

Composer Index

Bach, Johann Sebastian
    Musette, 93
Bartók, Béla
    Springtime Song, 230–231
Beethoven, Ludwig van
    Für Elise, 245–246
    Ode to Joy, 26
    Shepherd's Song, 32

Diabelli, Antonio
    Melody, 56
Duke, David
    The Cathedral in the Snow, 235–236

Evans, Lee
    Razzle Dazzle, 77–78

Finney, Ross Lee
    Seashore, 234

Goedicke, Alexander
    Russian Dance, 167
Gurlitt, Cornelius
    Vivace, 244

Joplin, Scott
    The Entertainer, 248–249

Kabalevsky, Dmitri
    Dance, 243
    A Little Joke, 232
    Moving Around, 243
Köhler, Louis
    Melody, 242

Leontovych, Mykola
    Carol of the Bells, 210–211
Lowry, Robert
    Shall We Gather at the River, 94

Mier, Martha
    Just Struttin' Along, 226–227

Olson, Lynn Freeman
    Razz-Ma-Tazz, 252

Pachelbel, Johann
    Canon, 130–132
Peirick, Aaron
    Aaron's Song, 106–107
Pierpont, J. S.
    Jingle Bells, 120–121

Rebikoff, Vladimir
    The Bear, 228–229
Robertson, Rick
    A First Nocturne, 250–251

Schubert, Franz
    Écossaise, 247

Türk, Daniel Gottlob
    March, 242

Vivaldi, Antonio
    Spring, 107–108

Wohlfahrt, Heinrich
    Prelude, 212–213

Subject Index

ABA musical form, 145–147
AB musical form, 149
Accent sign, 72
Accompaniment patterns
    Alberti bass, 27, 197–198, 199
    arpeggio, 144–145, 152
    block-chord, 152, 169, 198–199, 214
    broken-chord, 215
    drone bass, 51, 98
    waltz, 166, 170
Adagio, 65
Alberti, Domenico, 197
Alberti bass accompaniment pattern, 27,
    197–198, 199
Alla breve (cut time), 121
Allegretto, 65
Allegro, 65
Andante, 65
Arpeggiated chords, 177
Arpeggiated inversions, 184–185
Arpeggio accompaniment pattern,
    144–145, 152
A tempo, 105

B♭, 191
Barber, Samuel, 229
Bar lines, 4
Baroque period, 89, 132
Bass (F) clef, 40, 42
Beams, 90
Beats, 4
Binary form (two-part/AB form), 149
Black keys
    three groups, 7, 8
    two groups, 6, 7
    white keys located with, 12–14
Block-chord accompaniment pattern, 152,
    169, 198–199, 214
Blocked inversions, 184–185
Blue note, 238
Blues, 219–222
    12-bar, 219, 238–239
Blues scale, 220

B♭ major chord, 193–196
Bottom note, 112, 115
Brahms, Johannes, 47
Broken-chord accompaniment pattern,
    215
Brubeck, Dave, 97

Cage, John, 229
C⁷ chord, 193–196
C-D-E groups (white keys), 12–13
C five-finger position, 23–25
Change-of-tempo terms
    ritardando (rit.), 70
    a tempo, 105
Chopin, Frédéric, 3, 47, 102
Chord inversions, 183–185
Chord progressions
    C, F, and G⁷, 117
    C and F, 116
    C and G⁷, 112
    F, B♭, and C⁷, 196
    F and B♭, 195–196
    F and C⁷, 194–196
    G, C, and D⁷, 163
    G and C, 162–163
    G and D⁷, 160–161
Chords, *see also* major chords; minor
        chords; triads
    arpeggiated, 177
    C⁷, 193–196
    D⁷, 160–161, 163
    G⁷, 111–112, 117
    primary, 117
    seventh, 183
Chromatic scale, 98–99
Classical period, 27
Clefs, 40, *see also* bass clef; treble clef
Cliburn, Van, 5
C major chord, 104, 111–112, 117, 161–163
C major five-finger pattern, 87, 90, 98, 104
C major scale, 139–142
C minor chord, 103, 104
C minor five-finger pattern, 101, 102, 104

Common time, 24–25, 27
Contemporary period, 229
Contrary motion
　　C major scale played in, 141
　　G major scale played in, 159
　　harmonic minor scale played in, 205
Copland, Aaron, 229
Crescendo, 47
Cristofori, Bartolomeo, 3
Cut time *(alla breve)*, 121

Dal segno al fine (D.S. al Fine), 77
Damper pedal, 49
　　direct pedaling, 127–129
　　legato pedaling, 178–182
D⁷ chord, 160–161, 163
Decrescendo, 47
Diminished triads, 177
Diminuendo, 47
Direct pedaling, 127–129
D major chord, 105
D major five-finger pattern, 88, 94, 105
D minor chord, 105
D minor five-finger pattern, 105
Dorian mode, 33–36
Dotted half note, 4, 118
Dotted half rest, 118
Dotted quarter note, 118–123
Dotted quarter rest, 118
Double bar lines, 4
Downbeat, 53
Drone bass accompaniment pattern, 51,
　　98
Dynamic markings
　　crescendo, 47
　　decrescendo, 47
　　diminuendo, 47
　　forte (f), 10
　　fortissimo (ff), 76
　　mezzo forte (mf), 8–9
　　mezzo piano (mp), 8–9
　　pianissimo (pp), 76
　　piano (p), 10

Écossaise, 247
Eighth note, 90
8va, 70
Electronic keyboard, 220

F♯, 157
F clef, *see* bass clef
Fermata, 64
F-G-A-B groups (white keys), 13–14

15*ma*, 233
Fifths (inverval), 51
Fifth tone, 89, 103
Fingers, *see also* five-finger patterns
　　crossing over and under, 140
　　extension of, 143
　　flexing of, 2
　　numbers of, 3
　　position of, 2
　　substitution of, 145
First ending, 16
First inversion, 183
Five-finger patterns
　　blues, 220
　　C, 23–25
　　changing position, 124–126
　　G, 27–28
　　major (*see* major five-finger patterns)
　　minor (*see* minor five-finger patterns)
Flat sign, 67
F major chord, 104, 115, 117, 193–196
F major five-finger pattern, 88, 95, 104
F major scale, 191–193
F minor chord, 104
F minor five-finger pattern, 104
Forms, 145, *see also* binary form; ternary
　　form
Forte (f), 10
Fortissimo (ff), 76
Fourths (interval), 49, 183

G⁷ chord, 111–112, 117
G clef, *see* treble clef
Gershwin, George, 229
G five-finger position, 27–28
G major chord, 104, 160–161, 162–163
G major five-finger pattern, 87, 91, 104
G major scale, 157–159
G minor chord, 104
G minor five-finger pattern, 103, 104
Grand staff, 40–41
Gregorian chant, 20

Half note, 4, 118
Half rest, 29, 118
Half step, 85
Handel, George Frederick, 132
Hands
　　melodies divided between two, 29
　　playing arpeggiated chords with alter-
　　　nating, 177
　　position of, 2
Harmonic intervals, 43

Harmonic major scale, 204
Harmonic minor scale, 204–206
Harmonizing lead-line melodies, 133
    Alberti bass accompaniment, 199
    arpeggio accompaniment, 152
    block-chord accompaniment, 152, 169,
        198–199, 214
    broken-chord accompaniment, 215
    waltz accompaniment, 170
Harmonizing melodies, 111–136
Haydn, Franz Joseph, 27, 31
Horowitz, Vladimir, 241

i chord, 206
Improvisation
    Dorian mode, 35–36
    with drone bass accompaniment, 98
    open fifth, 79
    pentatonic, 18–19
    12-bar blues, 219, 238–239
Innovative notations, 233–234
Intervals, 43–44, 148–150
    fifths, 51
    fourths, 49, 183
    harmonic, 43
    melodic, 43
    octaves, 150
    seconds, 44–45
    sevenths, 150
    sixths, 148
    thirds, 45–46, 183
iv chord, 206

Jazz, 225–227

Keyboard
    overview, 6–8
    sitting at, 1–2
Key signatures
    B♭, 191
    F♯, 157
    flat sign, 67
    sharp sign, 70

Landmark notes, 40
Landmark pairs, 41–43
Lead lines, 133, see also harmonizing lead-
    line melodies
Legato, 14
Legato pedaling, 178–182
Leger lines, 40, 41
Line notes, 39, 44
Liszt, Franz, 47, 176, 197

Major chords, 89–90, 104–105
    B♭, 193–196
    C, 104, 111–112, 117, 161–163
    D, 105
    F, 104, 115, 117, 193–196
    G, 104, 160–161, 162–163
Major five-finger patterns, 86–89, 90,
    104–105
    C, 87, 90, 98, 104
    D, 88, 94, 105
    F, 88, 95, 104
    G, 87, 91, 104
Major scales, 139
    C, 139–142
    F, 191–193
    G, 157–159
    harmonic, 204
    in tetrachord position, 140
    triads of, 175–177
Measures, 4
Melodic intervals, 43
Melodies
    in C five-finger position, 23–25
    in G five-finger position, 27–28
    harmonizing, 111–136 (see also harmo-
        nizing lead-line melodies)
    in middle C position, 29
    playing using different positions,
        23–38
Metronome marking, 235
Mezzo forte (mf), 8–9
Mezzo piano (mp), 8–9
Middle C position, 29
Middle note, 112, 115
Minor chords, 103, 104–105
    C, 103, 104
    D, 105
    F, 104
    G, 104
    i, iv, and V⁷ in, 206
Minor five-finger patterns, 101–103,
    104–105
    C, 101, 102, 104
    D, 105
    F, 104
    G, 103, 104
Minor scales
    harmonic, 204–206
    relative, 203–204
Moderato, 65
Molto, 208
Mozart, Wolfgang Amadeus, 3, 27

Natural sign, 71
Neumes, 20
Notations
    beginnings of, 20
    innovative, 233–234
Note values, 4

Octaves
    defined, 12
    interval (eighths), 150
    playing in various, 61–65
Open fifth improvisation, 79
Ozone, Makoto, 79

Parallel motion
    C major scale played in, 142
    F major scale played in, 193
    G major scale played in, 159
    harmonic minor scale played in, 206
Pentatonic improvisation, 18–19
Pentatonic scale, 18
Phrase markings, 25–26
Pianissimo (pp), 76
Piano, background of, 3
Piano (p), 10
Pianoforte, 3
Pitches, *see* tones
Prelude, 207–213
Primary chords, 117

Quartal harmony, 235–237
Quarter note, 4, 118–123
Quarter rest, 29, 118

Ragtime, 223–225
Reading music, 39–60, 61–82
Relative minor scale, 203–204
Repeat sign, 16
Rests, 29, 118
Rhythm, 4
Ritardando (rit.), 70
Romantic period, 47
Root position, 183
Root (first) tone, 89, 103
Rounds, 28
Rubinstein, Arthur, 151

Salieri, Antonio, 31
Scales
    blues, 220
    chromatic, 98–99
    defined, 139

major (*see* major scales)
minor (*see* minor scales)
pentatonic, 18
Scarlatti, Domenico, 132
Scherzando, 232
Schnabel, Artur, 241
Schumann, Robert, 47
Second ending, 16
Second inversion, 183
Seconds (interval), 44–45
Sempre staccato, 197
Seventh chord, 183
Sevenths (interval), 150
Sharp sign, 70
Sixths (interval), 148
Slur markings, 25–26
Space notes, 39, 44
Staccato notes, 72
Staffs, 39, 40–41
Stravinsky, Igor, 229

Tchaikovsky, Peter, 47
Tempo, 65
Tempo markings, *see also* change-of-
    tempo terms
    adagio, 65
    allegretto, 65
    allegro, 65
    andante, 65
    moderato, 65
    scherzando, 232
Tenuto, 167
Ternary form (three-part/ABA form),
    145–147
Tetrachord position
    C major scale in, 140
    F major scale in, 192
    G major scale in, 158
    harmonic minor scale in, 204
    major scale in, 140
Thirds (interval), 45–46, 183
Third tone, 89, 103
Tied notes, 31–32
Time signatures
    $\frac{2}{2}$ (cut time), 121
    $\frac{2}{4}$, 102
    $\frac{3}{4}$, 29–30
    $\frac{4}{4}$ (common time), 24–25, 27
Tones, 6, 89, 103
Tonic, 87
Top note, 112, 115
Touch, playing by, 2
Transposition, 47

Treble (G) clef, 40, 41
Triads, *see also* chords
    diminished, 177
    of the major scale, 175–177
12-bar blues, 219, 238–239
Twentieth century classics, 228–232

Upbeat, 53

V^7 chord, 206

Waltz accompaniment pattern, 166, 170
Watts, André, 238
White keys, 6
    using, 11–12
    using black-key groups to locate,
      12–14
Whole note, 4
Whole rest, 29
Whole step, 86

CD Track List

DISC 1

Unit 1

1:1 Distant Shores (p. 9)
1:3 Saigon Traffic (pp. 10–11)
1:5 Remembering (p. 15)
1:7 Rock My Soul (pp. 16–17)
1:9 Sakura (p. 18)

Unit 2

1:10 Au Claire De La Lune (pp. 24–25)
1:12 Ode to Joy (Beethoven) (p. 26)
1:14 Whistle Daughter (p. 28)
1:16 A Jazz Waltz (p. 30)
1:18 Shepherd's Song (Beethoven) (p. 32)
1:20 Dorian Four (pp. 33–34)

Unit 3

1:21 Landmark Pairs (pp. 42–43)
1:23 Stepping Along (pp. 44–45)
1:25 Love Somebody (p. 46)
1:27 Gliding (p. 48)
1:29 Chimes Afar (p. 50)
1:31 Country Tune (p. 52)
1:33 Swing (p. 53)
1:35 When the Saints Go Marching In (pp. 54–55)
1:37 Melody (Diabelli) (p. 56)

Unit 4

1:38 Stepping Up in C (p. 62)
1:40 Stepping Down in C (p. 63)
1:42 Navajo Chant (pp. 64–65)
1:44 Dialogue (p. 66)
1:46 Shortenin' Bread (p. 68)
1:48 Latin Moves (p. 69)
1:50 Acaba (pp. 70–71)
1:52 Monday Blues (p. 72)
1:54 Ole! (p. 73)
1:56 Shoestring Boogie (pp. 74–75)
1:58 Fanfare (p. 76)
1:60 Razzle Dazzle (Evans) (pp. 77–78)

Unit 5

1:61 Casey Jones (p. 92)
1:63 Musette (Bach) (p. 93)
1:65 Shall We Gather at the River (Lowry) (p. 94)
1:67 Song of Praise (p. 95)
1:69 French Folk Song (pp. 96–97)

Unit 6

1:70 Reverie (p. 102)
1:72 Chickalileeo (p. 103)
1:74 Aaron's Song (Peirick) (pp. 106–107)
1:76 Spring (Vivaldi) (pp. 107–108)

Unit 7

1:77 Mary Ann (p. 113)
1:79 Bells of London (p. 114)
1:81 German Folk Song (p. 114)
1:83 Jingle Bells (Pierpont) (pp. 120–121)
1:85 Kum Ba Yah (pp. 122–23)
1:87 Perpetual Rock (pp. 124–125)
1:89 Time-Clock Blues (p. 126)
1:91 Moonlit Sea (p. 128)
1:93 Scottish Highlands (p. 129)
1:95 Canon (Pachelbel) (pp. 130–132)
1:96 Alleluia (p. 133)

DISC 2

Unit 8

2:1 Scale Study No. 1 (p. 142)
2:3 Scale Study No. 2 (p. 143)
2:5 Michael, Row the Boat Ashore (p. 144)
2:7 On Top of Old Smoky (p. 145)
2:9 Classic Twist (pp. 146–147)
2:11 Sixth Degree (p. 149)
2:13 Urubamba Majesty (p. 151)
2:15 Beautiful Brown Eyes (p. 152)

Unit 9

2:17 Jacob's Ladder (p. 164)
2:19 Angels We Have Heard on High (p. 165)
2:21 My Hat, It Has Three Corners (p. 166)
2:23 Russian Dance (Goedicke) (p. 167)
2:25 Amazing Grace (pp. 168–169)
2:26 Du, Du Liegst Mir Im Herzen (pp. 169–170)

Unit 10

2:28 Soaring (pp. 180–181)
2:30 Then and Now (p. 182)
2:32 Classic Dance (p. 186)

Unit 11

2:34 Auld Lang Syne (p. 196)
2:36 Ah, Vous Dirai-Je, Maman? (p. 198)
2:38 New River Train (pp. 198–199)

Unit 12

2:40 Moroccan Sands (p. 207)
2:42 Prelude (p. 208)
2:44 Scarborough Fair (p. 209)
2:46 Carol of the Bells (Leontovych) (pp. 210–211)
2:48 Prelude (Wohlfahrt) (pp. 212–213)
2:49 Ukrainian Folk Song (pp. 214–215)

Unit 13

2:51 Windy City Blues (p. 221)
2:53 Transcendental Blues (p. 222)
2:55 What Time? Ragtime (pp. 224–225)
2:57 Just Struttin' Along (Mier) (pp. 226–227)
2:59 The Bear (Rebikoff) (pp. 228–229)
2:61 Springtime Song (Bartók) (pp. 230–231)
2:63 A Little Joke (Kabalevsky) (p. 232)
2:65 Seashore (Finney) (p. 234)
2:67 Black and White (p. 237)

Unit 14

2:68 March (Türk) (p. 242)
2:70 Melody (Köhler) (p. 242)
2:72 Dance (Kabalevsky) (p. 243)
2:74 Moving Around (Kabalevsky) (p. 243)
2:76 Vivace, Gurlitt (p. 244)
2:78 Für Elise (Beethoven) (pp. 245–246)
2:80 Écossaise (Schubert) (p. 247)
2:82 The Entertainer (Joplin) (pp. 248–249)
2:84 A First Nocturne (Robertson) (pp. 250–251)
2:86 Razz-Ma-Tazz (Olson) (p. 252)
2:88 Wondering (Keveren) (pp. 253–254)